PUPPY STUFF

A CONCISE, INFORMATIONAL BABY BOOK

FOR TODAY'S BUSY PUPPY "PARENTS"

Jodi Alessandrini & Kathy Kinser

Illustrations by Diane M. Cape

Pallachip Publishing, Springfield, Illinois

Pallachip Publishing
P. O. Box 9677
Springfield, Il 62791-9677

Printed in the United States of America by Walsworth Publishing Company, Marceline, Missouri

Illustrations and cover by Diane M. Cape
Veterinary Sources: Louis Brad, DVM; Franklin A. Coble, DVM; Janet L. Hill, DVM; Gregory B. Hurst, DVM.

ISBN 0-9647465-6-5

10 9 8 7 6 5 4 3 2 1

First Printing - 97

TO SOME REAL DOGS!

To Chocolate Chip, also known as Chip, and Palla di Neve (ball of snow), also known as Nevi, whose "puppy stuff" inspired us to write this book. Thanks for shredding all the parts you didn't like.

And to Annie, Nicky, Tyler, and Darby for inspiring Diane to create such adorable drawings.

And to Lady, Goldie, Bootsie, Peaches, T. S., Ginger I, George Henry, Ginger II, Penny, Charlie, Laddie, Scratch, Frank, Gentle Tamsworth, Orville, Blu, Nisha, J. T., Curley, Pee Wee, Buttons, Libby, Katie and Cody for all the very lovely memories included in our book.

We love and cherish you all!

CHIP
"CHIEF SHREDDER"

NEVI
"ROVING SHREDDER"

"The Almighty, who gave the dog to be companion of our pleasures and our toil, hath invested him with a noble nature and incapable of deceit."

Sir Walter Scott

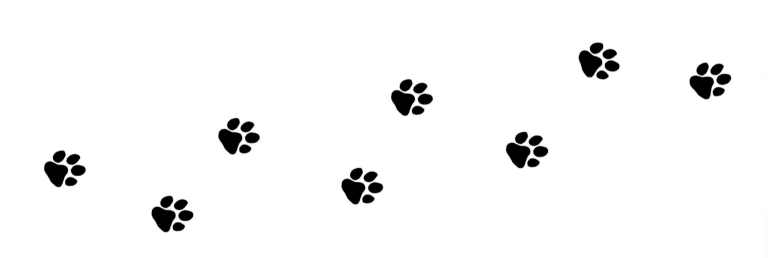

SPECIAL THANKS

To our veterinarian friends, for making us look smarter than we are

Louis Brad, DVM, is a 1986 graduate of the University of Illinois, College of Veterinary Medicine. He has practiced in Illinois, North Carolina and presently owns the Gunbarrel Veterinary Clinic in Boulder, Colorado. He is the advisor for a monthly magazine about ferrets. His prior work with the Southern Illinois Humane Society influenced his philosophy about the role of animals in our lives. Wayne and Garth, his two rescued office cats and Kumu, his house cat, have benefited from his philosophy.

Franklin A. Coble, DVM, is a 1970 graduate of the University of Illinois, College of Veterinary Medicine. He owns and operates Coble Animal Hospital in Springfield, Illinois which was established by his father, J. Porter Coble, DVM. His two black Labrador dogs, Tar and Puppy, accompany him to work everyday.

Janet L. Hill, DVM, is a graduate of the University of Missouri at Colombia. Upon graduation, she started practice in Boonville, Missouri. She is now in practice at Hurst Animal Hospital in Springfield, Illinois. She resides in Springfield with her husband, Jeff, their sons, Taylor and Drew, a collie named Cody and two cats, Oscar and Mattie. Oscar was dumped at her veterinary school and rescued by Janet. Mattie showed up at her front door one day and never left.

Gregory B. Hurst, DVM, is a 1984 graduate of the Univerisity of Illinois, College of Veterinary Medicine. He returned to his hometown of Springfield, Illinois to open his practice. He and his wife, Ann, have two children. Their family pets are a hedgehog called Sonic and a Jack Russell terrier named Lacey.

To our editing friends, for making us appear literate

Jim Agnew grew up the son of a zoo director. He lives with two dogs, three cats, two turtles, one hamster, one pigeon and his wife, Erin. He graduated Phi Beta Kappa from the Univeristy of Illinois with a degree in Creative Writing.

Jeri Heminghous is the owner of BrewHoppers By Mail, Broomfield, Colorado. She is also a Marketing Consultant with a Master's in Business Administration, University of Colorado at Boulder. She lives with her husband, Mark, and their cat, Gizmo.

Linda Kopecky was a college English teacher for many years before a recent move to the Illinois State Board of Education. She is an ardent Anglophile and gardener, who indulges these passions as time and finances allow.

John O'Halloran is a serious poet from Dublin, Ireland. He came to Sangamon State University at Springfield, Illinois, where he received a Master's Degree in English Literature. He is currently in Boston pursuing a writing career.

To our illustrator friend, for giving life to our text

Diane M. Cape has been owned by a succession of wonderful dogs. She currently lives with canines, Tyler and Darby, and husband, Chuck Cali. She is a graduate of Illinois State University, and has been an illustrator for more than twenty years.

To our computer friends, for making us look terrific

Jan Hayes is a Senior in the Managment Information Systems Department of Kerber, Eck & Braeckel. She formatted our book beautifully and very patiently and precisely placed 829 paw prints on these pages.

Becky McVay is a graphic artist who applied striking color to Diane's drawings. Becky, husband Keith, their four children, two hedgehogs, a guinea pig and a cockatiel are allowed to share the household with Alice D., a loving but maniacal kitten, who promptly took over the McVay home after being adopted by them.

To our accounting friend, for keeping us in the black

Joseph A. Alessandrini, Certified Public Accountant, partner in the regional CPA firm of Kerber, Eck and Braeckel. He is a very supportive husband who always thinks up clever and innovative solutions to problems.

To our other friends, for encouraging us to keep writing

Julie Alessandrini, daughter extraordinaire. She is a patient, friendly teacher and a real dog lover.

Pat Kendal, affectionately known as The Fishlady, is the self-published author of <u>The Fishlady's Basic Seafood Cookbook</u>, <u>The Fishlady's Holiday Entertaining Cookbook</u>, and <u>The Fishlady's Forever Dieter's Cookbook</u>. With a little help from Flip, The Fish, she teaches people to cook fish without intimidation.

Dr. David E. Kinser is a Springfield ophthalmologist and an all around great husband and man of few words. His most memorable words are, "Just write it!"

David H. Kinser, Kathy and Dave's son, is a 1992 graduate of Pomona College in Claremont, California. In his spare time he has helped edit our manuscript.

Lara Kinser, Kathy and Dave's daughter, is a recent graduate of Colorado State University. She owns a six pound cat named Frazzle and a beautiful 120 pound, Malamute named J.T., who is her constant canine companion.

Cheryl White has always been a puppy parent. She has owned a series of female toy poodles. One of her poodles, Buttons, grew up with her two sons and lived to the ripe old age of seventeen. Presently, she and her husband dote on Libby, a coal-black poodle, who is a bundle of love and adventure.

CONTENTS

PAWS to consider

POEMS

MY INFORMATION

MY PHOTOS

INTRODUCTION

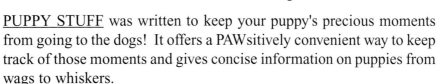

<u>PUPPY STUFF</u> was written to keep your puppy's precious moments from going to the dogs! It offers a PAWsitively convenient way to keep track of those moments and gives concise information on puppies from wags to whiskers.

The "PUPpourri" pages provide space for recording, in chronological order, puppy's progress, special events, best moments, medical records and awards. In addition, there are ample spaces for mounting those fabulous, fetching fotos of your wonderful, winsome whelp.

The "PAWS to consider" sections succinctly cover a wide variety of puppy care topics. Puppy related poetry is sprinkled throughout the book for a lighthearted view of your puppy from yet another perspective. Plus, a BONEus bookmark is provided so you won't have to dog-ear the pages.

<u>PUPPY STUFF</u> is based on knowledge the authors gained from years of dog-raising experience. In addition, the book has been reviewed by several veterinarians. <u>PUPPY STUFF</u> is easy to read, with information uniquely presented from the puppy's point of view. The book was created to capture the delights of puppyhood and beyond, and to offer a practical puppy care reference guide.

From two dog lovers to another, best wishes for enjoying all the "puppy stuff" your pup will provide.

Who waits to greet me at the door?
Who leaps up when my spirits soar?

Who sees my face and thinks it's dear?
Whose wiggle says, "I'm glad you're here?"

Who loves me when I look a mess?
Whose nose gives me a wet caress?

Who doesn't care if I should snore?
Who never thinks that I'm a bore?

Who sits with me to watch t.v.?
Whose chin is resting on my knee?

Who's at my feet as I sip wine?
Who gazes up to watch me dine?

Who gets a bite and begs for more?
Who helps to clean the kitchen floor?

Who's pleased to live, and lives to please?
Who's happy with a hug or squeeze?

MY PUPPY!

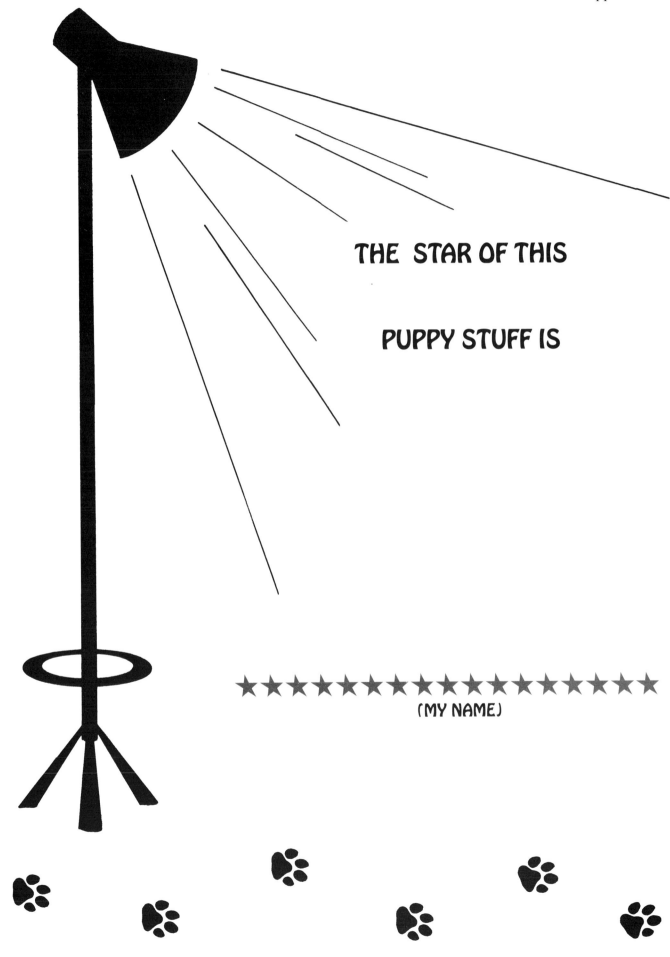

THE STAR OF THIS

PUPPY STUFF IS

★★★★★★★★★★★★★★★★★★★★★★

(MY NAME)

THE COMMITMENT

The commitment you make when you bring home a pup,
Is your **PROMISE** to care for it; **NEVER GIVE UP**!

Every year there are too many dogs put to sleep,
All because of a promise their owners won't keep.

So honor your promise remembering please,
To obey city leash laws; pay licensing fees.

Keep vet visits current, and shots up to date,
And neuter or spay if there's no plan to mate.

A fenced yard is fine, though it's not quite enough;
Include a name tag with your new puppy's stuff.

Secure puppy's space, it is wise to be smart,
For some puppies love mailmen a la carte!

Obedience training. What a positive tool!
You can teach pup at home or attend puppy school.

When puppy grows into a well-behaved pet,
It's just one of many rewards you will get.

Like friend and companion, a dog that is true,
Good natured, and happy; a credit to **YOU**!

PAWS to consider

YOUR COMMITMENT. I am Canis familiaris. As your friend, I greet you with high spirits. As your confidant, I know how to keep a secret. As your protector, I bark to alert you when strangers are near. As your pet, I respond to your authority and kindness by accepting you as my leader. As your companion, I am a trusted and valued member of your family. As your friendly advocate, I inspire conversation from complete strangers and thereby help you establish new friendships. As your walking partner, I promote your physical health through exercise. As a stimulus for fun and laughter, I help reduce your emotional and mental stress. As your hunting partner, I am ideally suited for tracking prey.

By recognizing my value as companion, protector, hunter and beast of burden, primitive peoples gave me a position of importance nearly equal to that of the gods. Down through the centuries, Canis familiaris has earned a reputation of trust and fidelity due to our ability to be intensely loyal to one owner. Historically, famous dogs have shown that we can overcome seemingly impossible odds in demonstrating our loyalty.

Thanks to your efforts, my potential for good is enormous. I am eyes for the sight impaired, ears for the hearing impaired, arms and legs for the physically challenged, companion for the elderly, motivation to live for the critically ill, partner for police and rescue teams, playmate for children and friend to all.

I know that you have given a great deal of thought to obtaining me. Please remember that I am trusting and innocent and should not be treated as a disposable product. Realistically, you can expect me to live for ten to eighteen years. I will consume some of your time, energy and financial resources. I must be fed, groomed, exercised, socialized, trained, and taken to the veterinarian regularly. I will need love and attention daily. From an adorable puppy, I have the potential, if trained and cared for properly, to become a dog worthy of your highest hopes.

Unfortunately, I have heard that millions of dogs are abused, neglected, or abandoned every year and, unless they are rescued, will most likely die lonely, miserable deaths. If at any time, you find that your expectations about dog ownership were unrealistic or that you acquired me on impulse, please do not abandon me, for I cannot fend for myself. Please do the right thing! Return me to my original owner, or try to find a loving home for me. You could advertise in the newspaper, but make sure I am going to a good home. Often bulletin boards at veterinary clinics or your local Humane Society have names of people seeking my type or breed. You could take me to the Humane Society with a donation to cover my costs until my new home is found. As a <u>very</u> <u>last</u> option, take me to my veterinarian and have me mercifully put to sleep. Remember, I trust you to take care of me. I am your Canis familiaris!

PETiculars

_____
MY NAME

My owner chose this name because _____

G̶w̶e̶n̶d̶o̶l̶y̶n̶
Z̶i̶p̶
➤ ANNIE

_____

PAWS to consider

> **MY NAME.** What's in my name? Plenty! Two syllable words that end in a vowel, such as Fido or Louie, are easiest for me to understand. One syllable names can be confused with one syllable commands, such as sit. Once you have chosen my name, be consistent. Avoid confusing me by using other names or terms of endearment. Strengthen the bond between us by talking often to me using my name.

My breed _____

My distinctive markings _____

My date of birth _____ I am a male/female (circle one)

My place of birth _____ (if known)

My weight at birth _____ (if known)

My present weight _____

Mom's Name _____ (if known)

Dad's Name _____ (if known)

My new owner's name(s) _____

My new home address _____

My age upon arriving at my new home _____

I was purchased from _____

My owner chose me because _____

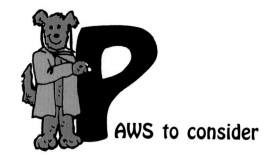

PAWS to consider

SELECTING A VETERINARIAN. Seek recommendations, and then make an appointment with the veterinarian of your choice. During the visit, consider the following:

- Does the veterinarian take time to answer your questions and explain procedures and options in an understandable way?
- Is he/she familiar with my breed and my peculiarities?
- Does he/she seem interested in keeping up with new procedures and technologies?
- Does he/she handle me gently?
- Does he/she practice preventive medicine?
- Is the facility close enough and available in case I have an emergency? If unavailable, for example, late at night - is there an acceptable alternative such as an animal emergency center?
- Is the veterinary facility clean?

VETERINARY VISITS. Take me to my veterinarian when I have any of the following problems:

- Lameness, difficulty standing, lying down or walking, broken bones, sprains, burns, wounds or other injuries
- Poisoning
- Skin rashes or lumps on or under the skin
- Foul odor from the ears or constant head shaking
- Excessive discharge from the nose or eyes
- Sores in the mouth
- Excessive hair loss, mange, dry coat or dandruff
- Sudden loss of appetite, lack of interest in water, excessive thirst or sudden weight loss or gain
- Lack of energy or change in personality
- Abnormal bowel movements, blood in the stool or urine
- Persistent coughing
- Difficulty or inability to control urination - it is not abnormal if I become excited and make a puddle.
- Tenderness or pain when touched
- Vomiting blood or excessive vomiting
- Loss of consciousness, difficulty breathing or choking
- Seizures
- Frostbite or heatstroke
- Shock (unresponsive pupils or complete immobility)

PUPPIES AND DOGS NEED PROFESSIONAL VETERINARY CARE!

AWS to consider

MY VETERINARIAN

Name _____

Address _____

_____

_____

Phone _____

The following is a suggested schedule of inoculations and tests. For specific information, consult my veterinarian.

6 weeks:	distemper
9 weeks:	distemper/hepatitis/parvovirus/coronavirus
9 weeks:	bordetella
9 weeks:	take fecal sample to veterinarian to test for worms, continue yearly or as needed
3 months:	distemper/hepatitis/parvovirus/coronavirus, then yearly
3 months:	parainfluenza, then yearly
3 months:	leptospirosis, then yearly
3 months:	bordetella, then yearly
3 months:	Lyme inoculation (where applicable) two vaccinations are given 3 weeks apart, followed by yearly boosters
4 months:	rabies with boosters every 1-3 years, depending on state law

Consult my veterinarian about the proper time to start heartworm preventative. It is usually given daily or monthly, year round. An annual blood test for heartworm is started at one year of age. Other inoculations may be recommended by my veterinarian based on your location and my breed.

We puppies and dogs should see our veterinarians once or twice a year, or when we have a problem. You and my veterinarian are now **partners** in promoting my good health! The following are a few suggestions for successful visits to my veterinarian.

- Tell the receptionist the nature of our visit when making an appointment.
- Make a list of questions for the veterinarian before our visit, and be prepared to answer questions about my health.
- Ask for instructions in writing about my care and medications. If you do not understand the instructions, ask for clarification before we leave.

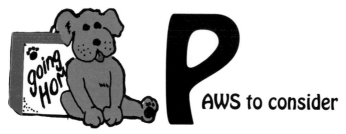

PAWS to consider

MY NEW HOME. Adjusting to a new environment is stressful for me. The holiday season is an especially difficult time to introduce me to my new home, since this is a hectic time for everyone. If I am intended to be a gift, it is best to bring me home the day after Christmas so I am not exhausted by too much attention or neglected in the excitement of Christmas day. Instead, why not gift wrap a puppy related item or gift certificate for the intended recipient? Include a note saying that I will arrive soon. My first impressions of my new home are important, and I will need your full attention for the first few days. Remember, I am just a baby who has recently been separated from my mom and littermates.

Before bringing me home, take time to prepare children for my arrival. When picking me up from the breeder or pet store, take an old dish towel with you. Ask permission to place the towel with my kennel mates for a few minutes to absorb their scent. At home, place the towel in my bed and I will be comforted by the scent. Secure my medical records before leaving my previous owner.

During **the first week**, the following suggestions are helpful for my successful adjustment:

- Establish a routine. We puppies like to be creatures of habit and will grow into more secure and confident dogs when we can rely on a regular daily routine.
- Give me plenty of rest and quiet. I may become frightened and lonely, so try not to leave me alone in the house at any time during the first two days.
- Try to keep me from socializing with other household pets. Other pets might contract an illness from me or vice versa. After I have been immunized by my veterinarian, introduce me to the other pets gradually and with your constant supervision. Give the other pets plenty of attention so they will not be jealous.
- Keep a watchful eye on my eating and drinking habits.
- Feed me the same food I have been eating. If you decide to change foods, do so gradually. (See PAWS to consider/FEEDING, page 33.)
- Do not permit me to remain outside when temperatures are extremely hot or cold.
- Put a battery operated ticking clock and/or a battery operated radio, on low volume, near my bed to keep me company when I am lonely.
- Supervise small children's time with me, and do not permit them to carry me since they may drop me.
- Take me for a veterinary exam. Bring my medical records as well as a fecal sample to test for parasites.
- Check state and local laws concerning dog ownership.

Note: It is not wise to ship me by air until I am at least three months old. (See PAWS to consider/CAR SAFETY AND TRAVEL, page 63.)

PUPpourri

Before coming to my new home, I was examined by my breeder's veterinarian who left the following advice for my new owner:

_____

_____

To make me feel at home, my owner bought the following for me:

_____

_____

Shortly after acquiring me, my owner took me to my new veterinarian.
(See PAWS to consider/MY VETERINARIAN, page 17 for complete list of immunizations and MY HEALTH CARE RECORD, page 130.)

My veterinarian gave my owner the following advice:_____

_____

During my exam, I yelped, winced, shook, was "cool," tried to bite the vet (circle one) or I

_____

I was checked for worms and was found to have _____

I must take the following medications:_____

_____

for_____

at the following times:_____

When the visit was over, my vet gave me _____

My owner gave me a big hug, a treat, my favorite toy, a "good boy", "good girl", (circle one)

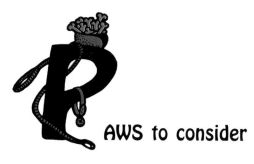

AWS to consider

SUPPLIES. Supplies I will need:

- **A bed.** My bed can be either a commercial wire or solid plastic crate, a box with a rug to sleep on or just a blanket or rug. We puppies tend to shred pillow beds, so it is a good idea to wait until we are older for this type of bed. For the same reason, a blanket with filling should not be used. If I am using a box, be sure that it has no staples or other objects that I can pull off and swallow. Fringed blankets or rugs should not be used because I can pull off the fringe and entangle myself. Note: "Puppy" is my name, and chewing is my game, so don't use a rug or blanket that is a family heirloom. If I am eventually going to become an outdoor dog, I will need a **shaded kennel or shaded insulated dog house** with plenty of room for exercise. A bed of hay inside the kennel or dog house will be needed for warmth during winter months. When using only a kennel, provide a covered insulated area to protect me from rain or cold weather. Although it is fine to kennel me for short periods, I should not be outdoors and alone throughout my life. (See PAWS to consider/SLEEPING, page 37.)

NAIL clippers
Leash
brush
TREATS
Shampoo
bowls

- **A feeding bowl and a water bowl** large enough for me to use as I grow bigger. The bowls should be made of heavy ceramic or stainless steel with weighted bottoms because we puppies love to tip our bowls over and play in the water. You will find that it stops being cute after the first two or three times. For long-eared dogs, there are feeding bowls designed so that their ears won't drag through their food. A flat-nosed dog will need flat, shallow dishes, while a longer muzzled dog will need deeper containers. Elevated bowls are available for long-legged puppies.

- **A six foot long leash, a buckle collar or harness**. These should be made of soft leather or nylon. A leather leash is easier on your hands. Do not use chain link leashes because they may injure you or me. My leash should be sturdy enough for my weight, so I cannot break it and run off. Wait until I am leash trained before using one of the long retractable leashes. Also, check your city laws since some cities prohibit the use of long leashes. To assure proper collar fit, measure the circumference of my neck and add two inches. Continue to adjust the size of my collar as I grow. A rolled collar is best if I am long-haired. To assure proper harness fit, measure the circumference of my body immediately behind my forelegs and add two inches.

- **Grooming tools.** A wire brush <u>or</u> natural bristle brush and a blunt wide-toothed comb are best for a long-haired dog. However, the hair of some breeds may tear when using a wire brush. A hound glove (a mitt with short bristles in the palm), metal comb or curry brush is best for a short-haired dog. Check with a pet supply store, my veterinarian or breeder for the right type of grooming tools for me. (See PAWS to consider/GROOMING, page 48.)

- **A nail clipper or file** if you are planning to trim my nails. (See PAWS to consider/ PETicures, page 50.)

- **Products for cleaning my teeth** include sterile gauze pads and oral cleaning solution, or a canine toothbrush and toothpaste. (See PAWS to consider/DENTAL HYGIENE, page 51.)

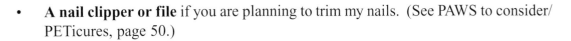

- **Bathing Products.** Flea and tick shampoo and regular canine shampoo for other times. Clean towels for my use only. Cotton balls and ear cleaning solution for ear care. (See PAWS to consider/BATHING, page 44.)

- **Odor remover** for the home and my fur.

- **Blunt-nosed scissors or hair trimming equipment,** if my breed requires these.

- **Prescribed medications and vitamins**, if needed.

- **A doggy first aid kit or first aid book.** (See SOME DOGGONE GOOD ADVICE, page 136.)

- **An identification tag** with my name, your name, address and phone number. The tag should be securely attached to my collar. If I am lost, I want to make sure someone can help me find my way home. (See PAWS to consider/ LOST PUPPIES, page 88.)

- **Dog biscuits and treats**. Check the moisture content in the treats. If the moisture content exceeds 12%, the treats may cause diarrhea for some of us. Treats should be given in moderation.

- **Toys** that are safe for chewing and for playtime. Balls should not be small enough for me to swallow. Check squeak toys to make sure I cannot pull the squeaker out and swallow it. Toys should be appropriate to my size.

- **A dog safety harness** for car travel and a **canine life preserver** for boating. (See PAWS to consider/CAR SAFETY AND TRAVEL, page 63.)

Supplies that would be nice to have:

- **A spoon and fork** to be used for my food only. **A rubber mat** under both food and water bowls to prevent messes.

- **A choke collar** to be used during training sessions <u>only</u>. It should not be used before I am six months old because it may injure my trachea. I should never wear a choke collar when I am unattended, since the collar could become entangled and strangle me.

- **Products to prevent me from chewing** my fur and scratching my skin, such as, Bitter Lime™ by Four Paws. (Nevi's "parents" sprayed it on furniture and cords and discovered it prevented him from chewing them.) Always test a product on a small unseen area of fabric before using.

- **A non-breakable rectal thermometer.**

- **Disposable pads for housetraining.**

- **A book** on my specific breed.

- **A gate** to block doorways or stairways. You can purchase a gate designed for dogs from a pet supply store or pet catalog.

- **A <u>Puppy Stuff</u> toy box** (see order form at back of book).

MY FIRST PHOTO IN MY NEW HOME

MY BIRTH OR REGISTRATION CERTIFICATE
OR ANOTHER PHOTO

Paws to consider

CHILDREN AND PUPPIES.

I take to children like a bear to honey. I am a ready playmate and friend. I comfort children when they are sad or insecure, and I am added joy during their good times.

Prepare the children for my arrival by teaching them that I am an addition to their family and <u>not</u> a toy. I must be treated gently and kindly. They should be taught how to be responsible pet owners. After I arrive, give all children in the household, depending on their ages and capabilities, the responsibility of taking care of one of my needs, such as feeding or exercise. By caring for me, children learn responsibility and compassion. Let the children accompany us when we visit the veterinarian, so they can comfort me and be a part of my total care. Take the children with us to obedience school, so that they can learn first hand how to train me.

For the first month or two, I will tire easily. When I become tired, take me to my bed and allow me to rest quietly. Children should be taught not to bother me when I am sleeping. If I am awakened suddenly, I may be disoriented and try to protect myself by biting. Likewise, I should be left alone when I am eating.

Teach the children how to play with me without hurting or injuring me. No squeezing, pinching, poking, falling on top of me or trying to ride me. Explain to the children that they would not like to be treated this way or would not like to be bitten, if I defended myself. Also, children should not shout at me, startle me, make intimidating movements toward me, pull my hair or tease me. All of these will either frighten me or make me hostile toward them. I should not be expected to pull wagons or sleds or be ridden. If I am the kind of dog that is intended to pull sleds, wait until I am older and trained for that task. Just as I should be taught not to take the children's toys, they should be taught not to take mine. Teach the children how to keep me safe when I am outdoors. They should not play with me in areas that are unfenced or near streets. We puppies are not really fond of being carried improperly. Children should be shown the proper way to carry me by placing one hand under my chest and the other under my hindquarters to lift me.

I want to learn how to interact positively with all members of my new family. If trained properly, I will be successful in adjusting to family members regardless of their ages. However, I may not understand when a baby cries, coos or waves its arms. I may become anxious or aggressive. Introduce me gradually to an infant, and monitor our activities together. Be sure to keep soiled diapers out of my reach. A toddler, especially one who screams shrilly, can unintentionally irritate me, and I may either try to run away or bite. In fact, do not leave any child alone with me whom I might harm or who might harm me. Do not allow a young child to hold the leash when taking me for a walk. It would be very traumatic for the child if I suddenly broke away and was injured.

Throughout my life, if you continue to teach the children to be responsible dog owners, I will be their devoted friend for life.

I greet you in my special way,
With wagging tail and eyes so bright.
My puppy joy is unrestrained;
My body wiggles in delight!

Your happy voice, your gentle touch,
Are just what I've been waiting for;
I only know my life begins,
When you come running through the door!

I don't care if we're in the chips,
Or out of luck and destitute;
My wealth is knowing I'm all yours,
And that our friendship's absolute!

BECAUSE I'M YOUR PUPPY!

MY PAW PRINTS

To make prints, use food coloring or other non-toxic material. Make prints on separate pieces of paper. Affix to this page using glue in stick form. Be sure to rinse my feet afterwards.

FORE LEFT   **FORE RIGHT**

HIND LEFT   **HIND RIGHT**

SNIP OF MY HAIR

PHOTOS OF ME WITH MY NEW FAMILY

TWO TO THREE MONTHS

I weigh _____ I am _____tall.
(measure from floor to top of shoulder)

My owner bought these supplies for me: _____

_____

_____

To spoil me, my owner bought: _____

_____

_____

This month I've learned: _____

_____

_____

I first wore my collar at _____ months.
(Collars should not be used until the age of eight weeks because my trachea can be easily injured).

I recognized my name at _____ months.

I recognized my family at _____ months.

My favorite toys: _____

_____

I amuse myself by _____

_____

I bark at_____

PHOTOS OF ME DOING ADORABLE PUPPY STUFF

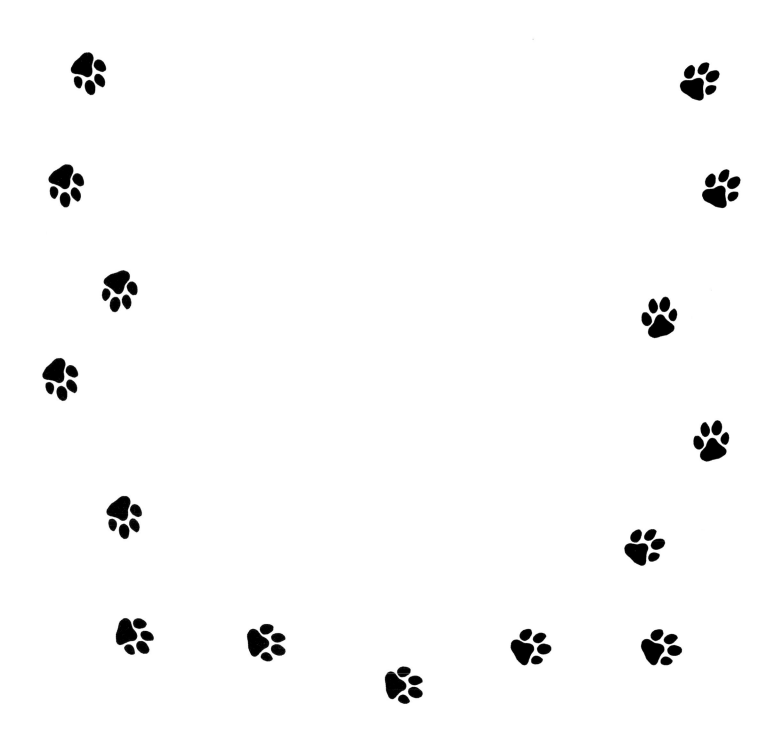

SAFETY. Make it difficult for me to be injured or get into trouble. Protect me and your belongings by looking at the house and yard from my level and removing or covering any potentially dangerous objects. The following are some suggestions for puppy-proofing my home and yard:

- Take up any small area rugs if I chew on them.

- Block electrical outlets. Tape electrical wires and cords (including phone cords) to the floor or baseboard.

- Secure loose drapery cords so I do not become entangled.

- Remove all plants within my reach. Some are poisonous. (See SOME DOGGONE GOOD ADVICE, page 138.) Grannick's Bitter Apple®, a bio-degradable product, can be safely sprayed on all plants and keeps me from chewing them. Do not use any poisonous substances, such as slug poison, in areas where I can reach them. Ask lawn service personnel how soon I can safely go outside after they have treated the grass or bushes. Read the safety instructions on all garden products you use.

- Remove all toxic substances from my area, including automobile products. Remove any antifreeze spills because their sweet taste will attract me. A new antifreeze product called Sierra® is on the market that is made with propylene glycol instead of ethylene glycol. It is less toxic to animals. For more information call, Safe Brands Corporation at 1-800-289-7234.

- Remove anything dangerous that I might chew and swallow. Of special concern are cigarette butts, aspirin substitutes, sharp or glass objects, and chocolate (which contains theobromine, a substance that is toxic to dogs). As a puppy, I will chew anything I can get my jaws on. It is natural for me to chew. Check children's toys for parts that I might pull off and swallow. Pet toys with squeakers may not be safe, since I may be able to remove the squeaker and swallow it. Replace my toys as soon as they start to fall apart. Yarn, string, sewing thread and continuous filament carpeting may strand out and cause an intestinal blockage.

- Remove valuable and breakable objects from my area.

- Keep closet and cabinet doors closed.

- Do not light fires or candles where I can reach them. Cover all fireplaces with screens. Protect me from barbecue grills and hot oven doors.

- Block stairways, especially those going down.

- Do not let me socialize with other pets until I have had all of my inoculations. It takes one to two weeks after a vaccine is given to activate immunity.

- Keep Christmas trees, packages and ornaments out of my reach. The water at the base of the tree can be toxic to me.

- Remove all plastic bags from my area. I could suffocate if I crawled into a plastic bag or choke on pieces I have torn from the bag.

- Keep second story windows without screens and low sills closed so I cannot fall out. Secure screens so I cannot push my way through them. Secure high balcony posts so I cannot squeeze through them. If I am a small dog, do not leave me unattended on a table or high place where I might jump off and break a bone.

- Place tape, drapes or shades across glass doors or windows. Often we dogs have difficulty perceiving clear glass as a barrier. We may crash into it or through it if we see something exciting on the other side.

- Fence the yard, using safe sturdy materials. The fence should be high enough so that I cannot jump over it. The fence will keep me safe and keep other animals out that might hurt me. Put a sign on the gates, reminding workers and others to keep the gate closed so I cannot wander out of my yard.

- Cover swimming pools and keep me away from ponds.

- Remove broken glass from the yard.

- Remove my fecal material frequently. Parasites flourish in feces.

- Securely cover all garbage cans, or remove them from my reach.

- Never leash me in an area where I may become entangled or possibly hang myself. Keep me on a leash and away from traffic when walking with me.

- Secure "animal on premises" stickers to the front and back doors of our house. In case of a fire, this will alert the firemen to my presence. If we move to another home, be sure to remove the stickers from the doors of the old house. We would not want the firemen spending time searching for me when I am no longer there.

- Put all toilet covers down, or I may be tempted to drink from the toilets. Toilet bowl cleaners are toxic.

- Keep all soiled diapers, baby bottles and bottle nipples out of my reach.

PUPpourri

I eat _____ times a day, in the _____, with _____

I eat _____ chow.

My favorite treat is _____

I get a treat when _____

_____

My favorite "people food" is _____ (In spite of my owner's best efforts to keep me on a canine diet, I discovered "people food.")

I got into a box of _____, a can of _____,

a bag of _____, a dish of _____

This is what happened: _____

_____

_____

My owner said, _____

_____

_____

In spite of my "discoveries," my owner still thinks I am _____

_____

_____

I responded to the word "no" at _____ months, when I was about to _____

_____

_____

PAWS to consider

FEEDING. Unlike humans, I have only one to two years to grow up to be big and strong. It is, therefore, important to choose a high quality, nutritionally complete <u>puppy</u> food for me during the first year and a nutritionally balanced <u>dog</u> food thereafter. Since I may have a sensitive tummy, feed me the same food that was fed to me by the breeder or pet store and on the same schedule. I can become a finicky eater if my food is changed too quickly or too often. After a week, if you wish to change my type of puppy food, introduce the new food slowly, mixing it with the food you are already giving me. Observe my bowel movements. If the stool is loose or I am straining, my diet is being changed too rapidly.

If you choose a canned puppy food, always refrigerate the unused portion so it will not spoil. It is more flavorful when you allow the unused portion to warm to room temperature before feeding me. If you choose a semi-moist food, consult my veterinarian to make sure it does not contain an excess of sugar and chemicals. Dry dog food is the most nutritionally balanced, easiest to store and the most economical when bought in large quantities. It is usually better for my teeth. Keep stored dog food out of my reach. Add a teaspoon of cod liver oil or corn oil to my food every other day if I should develop dry skin during the winter months. Consult my veterinarian about the amount and type of food that is best for me, and whether I may need vitamins, minerals or other supplements.

Follow the feeding guidelines on the puppy food package, but be flexible! If I am a very active puppy, I may need more food. I may require four meals a day until I am six months old. Thereafter, feed me twice a day. Leave my food bowl down for twenty minutes. After twenty minutes, remove the bowl even if I have not eaten. This will teach me to eat at regular times and help you to estimate my elimination timetable. After eating, take me immediately to my designated potty area. When no one is home during the day, feed me early in the morning so I will have sufficient time for exercise and elimination before you leave for work. It is not wise to leave me alone for more than four hours, so make arrangements for someone to take me out to potty and give me a little tender loving care during the day. (See PAWS to consider/HOUSETRAINING, page 40, and SLEEPING, page 37.) After I am completely housetrained, you can consider making my daily allowance of food available to me at all times, but only if I am eating dry dog food. This is called free feeding. (See PAWS to consider/ONE YEAR AND BEYOND, page 116.)

Note: Sometimes deep-chested dogs develop a condition called bloat, which is a buildup of gas and fluid in the stomach. This condition causes distress and may lead to death. The dog will look like it has swallowed a basketball. This is a <u>strict emergency</u>. Take the dog to the nearest veterinarian at once. As a precaution, deep-chested dogs should be fed twice a day and not exercised for two hours before or after eating. Using elevated dishes for feeding, so the dog does not have to raise and lower its head while eating, keeps a dog from ingesting excessive amounts of air which can lead to bloat. Examples of deep-chested dogs are the Great Dane, Irish Setter, German Shepard, Boxer and Samoyed.

Giving me treats can spoil my appetite and prevent me from eating the nutritional foods I need for growth. I may beg for your left-over steak bones, but don't ever fall for that ploy! Natural bones are <u>never</u> a good idea. They can chip teeth, which become difficult to save and prone to abscess. Bones can also splinter causing gastrointestinal problems. Give treats only as a reward during training or for good behavior. A few dog biscuits, however, can be given each day to aid the teething process. This is especially important when I am being fed only moist food. Avoid giving me table scraps. At first, it may be adorable when I sit up and beg, but before long I may grow to be as tall as the table. Then you will find it difficult to keep me from stealing the steak right off your plate! Feeding me at the same time you are eating may cut down on my desire to beg for your food. Keep a slice of raw onion or lemon on the table, and if I start to beg, let me sniff one of these. Usually, we puppies do not like these odors. When we think that this is what you are eating, we will gladly leave you alone.

"People food" is not nutritionally balanced for me, and some foods, such as chocolate, can be toxic or even fatal. Feeding me "people food" will not make me love you more. What it will do is make me fat and ruin my teeth. A fatty diet is also a cause of flatulence. You are responsible for what I eat. You should not let me gain more than 10% over my ideal weight. My ribs should not show, yet you should be able to feel them without pressing too hard. Gaining too much weight is easy, but taking it off is <u>not</u>. Sound familiar?

Obesity can be caused by thyroid problems. If I have a weight problem even though I am being fed correctly and exercised regularly, consult my veterinarian. If he cannot find a thyroid problem, he may suggest a dog food lower in fat. Cooked rice makes a good filler while I am adjusting to the lower fat/calorie count. Sometimes we puppies become dirt eaters, which may indicate a nutritional deficiency or it may be just a bad habit. Always consult my veterinarian concerning dramatic weight gains or losses.

Cool, fresh water should be available to me at <u>all</u> times. I may develop an upset stomach when I drink a large amount of water immediately before or after exercise. Milk, which may cause diarrhea and allergies, is generally not good for me.

Make sure that my food and water bowls are always clean. Feed me in the same place and at the same times every day. Most importantly, always remember to mix my food with a generous helping of love!

MOOCH POOCH

She's coming from the grocery store;
I'll lie here on the kitchen floor.
She knows that I'm an omnivore,
   IN THE KITCHEN.

I'll just pretend to be asleep;
My sense of smell will help me keep,
In touch with rhythm, pulse and beat,
   IN THE KITCHEN.

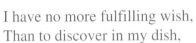

Aromas have such great appeal;
I hope fried chicken's my next meal,
And I will borrow, beg or steal,
   IN THE KITCHEN.

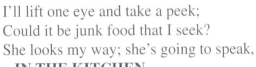

I have no more fulfilling wish,
Than to discover in my dish,
A lamb chop or filet of fish,
   IN THE KITCHEN.

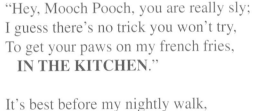
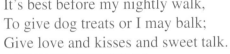

I'll lift one eye and take a peek;
Could it be junk food that I seek?
She looks my way; she's going to speak,
   IN THE KITCHEN.

"Hey, Mooch Pooch, you are really sly;
I guess there's no trick you won't try,
To get your paws on my french fries,
   IN THE KITCHEN."

It's best before my nightly walk,
To give dog treats or I may balk;
Give love and kisses and sweet talk.
   IN THE KITCHEN.

PUPpourri

My owner describes my personality as _____

My owner notices that I smile (yes/no) or look worried (yes/no).

I am happy when _____

I am unhappy when _____

I love it when someone scratches my _____

I tolerate _____

My nosiness gets me into trouble when _____

_____

I like to play with _____

My favorite games are _____

Other pet members in my family include _____

_____

Their names are _____

_____

The other pets think I am _____

I think the other pets are _____

I sleep in a _____, on a _____, under a

_____, by my _____, with my_____

First time I slept through the night was _____

When I sleep

    my nose/paws twitch _____

    I drool   _____

    I snore or bark   _____

    I dream   _____

    my tail wags

PAWS to consider

SLEEPING. Puppies and dogs sleep a lot. Regular sleep is very necessary to our health. When I am tired, where can I rest my weary head? I would prefer a crate designed for dogs or a pillow, rug or blanket placed in a box or small enclosed area. However, pillows, rugs or blankets are easy for me to rip. (See PAWS to consider/SUPPLIES, page 20.) I would like to have my bed or crate in the kitchen, family or utility room. These areas allow me to be near human activity without having to participate. Basements and garages are not good places because they can be too damp or lonely. While I am adjusting to your household, consider putting my crate or bed in your bedroom at night so I will feel safe knowing you are near. It is better not to let me sleep with the humans in the family while I am a puppy. We need to establish the master/dog relationship, and sleeping in your bed makes you seem like a pal. When I am resting, leave me alone. I am in my private place, and I should feel that it is safe and secure. When I am sleeping in my crate, do not allow children to poke their fingers through the wires or tease me. My crate or bed should be cleaned frequently to prevent parasites from accumulating. When we travel, my crate is very convenient. In the motel room, it will keep me out of mischief while you are sight-seeing and it will keep me safe while traveling in the car. (See PAWS to consider/CAR SAFETY, page 63.)

There are two types of crates; heavy-duty molded plastic, and wire. The plastic type allows for privacy and can be taken apart for ease in cleaning. The wire type provides better ventilation and visibility but does not allow for privacy. A large cloth can be placed over the wire crate when I require rest. Make sure that I cannot pull the cover through the wires, chew it and choke.

There are several benefits to crate usage. A crate offers me a sense of well-being. It is a safe place to rest after surgery, a temporary place to stay while traveling, and a help during housetraining. It also serves as my bed at night and a place where I can be confined for <u>short</u> periods while unattended. Giving me too much freedom, or the run of the house when I am young, is too much responsibility for me.

For all the many benefits crates offer, there are a few concerns, especially with the wire type. Make sure that the spaces between the wires are not large enough to trap my head or paw. When purchasing the crate, check to see that it does not have sharp edges or protrusions that might injure me. I should not be allowed to enter my crate wearing my training collar. If the collar became entangled on the wire, I could be strangled.

(The authors used crates as beds for their dogs, Chip and Nevi. They placed a rug inside each crate for warmth and comfort. The dogs instinctively considered the crate their den because their ancestors were denning animals. They felt secure and happy there. The authors were also happy, knowing that when they were away, Chip and Nevi were safe from harmful objects and were not shredding the drapes.)

Should you decide to use a crate, introduce me to it by opening the door and placing a treat inside. Allow me to go in, get the treat and come out. Repeat the process several times for a few days. Next, place my food bowl inside the crate. Leave the door of the crate open so I can come and go. After a few days place a treat inside. When I go inside, close the door for a few minutes. I might whine and cry, but do not open the door until I have quieted. Release and praise me. During my training period, be nearby where I can see you. Soon I will be happy to go to my crate to hide my toys or take a nap. When you expect me to go to my crate, always refer to it with the same words; for example, "Go to your crate." Or simply just say, "crate." On hearing those words, I will automatically go there.

My crate should be large enough for me to stand up, turn around and lie on my side, but not so large that I can soil one end and snooze at the other. You can create a partition in the crate making the space smaller. Removing the partition when I am larger eliminates the need to buy two crates. My natural instinct is to be clean. However, if I am left unattended for more than two hours at a time, I may soil my crate out of necessity. Under no circumstances should my crate be used to confine me for long hours without benefit of exercise and elimination. Furthermore, my crate should never be employed as a means of punishment. Such abuse of crate usage will only make me fearful and diminish our relationship.

Crates can make housetraining much easier. (See PAWS to consider/ HOUSETRAINING, page 40.) When using my crate for housetraining, you should be nearby to listen for whining sounds that indicate I need to relieve myself. When you are away all day, make arrangements for someone to let me out for elimination and exercise. If there is no one to let me out, place my crate, with its door open, in a confined area with an easy to clean floor. Place chew toys and treats inside, a tip proof bowl of water outside and plenty of newspapers on the floor. Then hope that I use the papers.

When you are supervising me during the day, leave the door of my crate open so I can come and go at will. As I outgrow my need for a crate, consider providing a rug or pillow bed filled with cedar chips. Cedar chips help reduce parasitic infestations. Make sure the chips are non-toxic.

If I become an outdoor dog, place newspapers with hay on top of them inside my dog house for warmth and comfort. Replace hay frequently. A dog house facing south or east with an offset door is best. In severe weather, I should be brought inside.

PHOTOS OF ME TAKING A SNOOZE

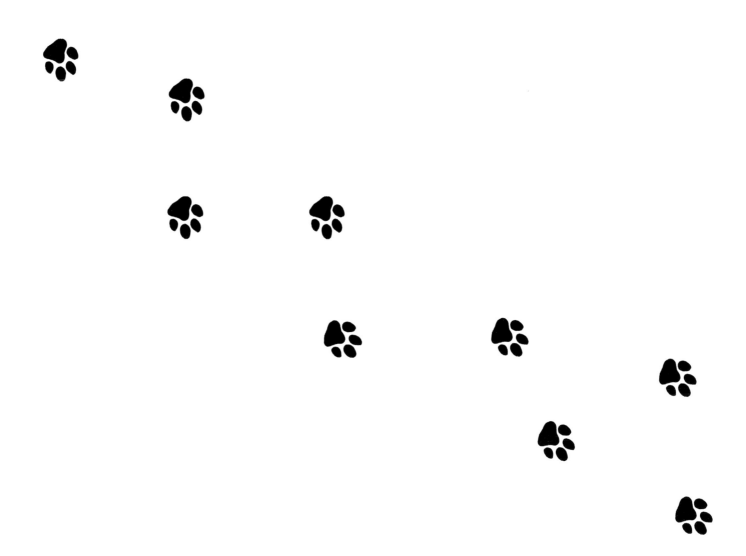

40

 AWS to consider

HOUSETRAINING. During housetraining, you have two options: indoors or outdoors. Begin housetraining as soon as I come home with you, but realize, during my early months, that my progress may be slow. I have limited bladder and bowel control until I am four or five months old. Until I gain control, take me outside or to my papered area often, and hope for the best. If you feed me at regular times during the day, you will be able to more accurately predict my elimination timetable. Do not free feed or change the type of food you are feeding me during my housetraining period. (See PAWS to consider/FEEDING, page 33.) If I become ill, discontinue housetraining until I am well.

Take me immediately to the <u>same spot</u> inside or outside at the following times:

- As soon as I wake in the morning
- After I wake from a nap
- If I appear uneasy or restless (whining, sniffing the floor or turning around in circles)
- After I eat or drink
- After playtime
- About every two hours between any of these activities
- Just before I go to bed at night

Use the same words every time you take me to my potty area; for example, "Go potty." The shorter the command, the better. When I am successful, give me generous amounts of praise. Have a treat handy to reward me. Frequently remove my feces from the yard, and if necessary, hose down the area or replace the mulch. Note: Urine can ruin grass, so you may want to create an area with mulch for me.

Indoor training requires using plenty of newspapers. Always place the papers in the same location where I have access to them. Begin by using lots of papers over a wide area. You may want to place a plastic tarp under the papers. Over time, gradually reduce the size of the papered area. When my actions show that I want to relieve myself, guide me gently to my potty area. Praise me when I am successful. Remove the soiled papers but leave a small piece on top of the fresh papers. The scent from this piece will attract me back to the same spot next time.

At first, paper training may seem more convenient than taking me outdoors, but it can be risky. I may decide to sidetrack the papers for your favorite plant or chair. If you have the habit of relaxing on the living room floor while reading the Sunday paper, you could be in for quite a surprise! However, if we live on the tenth floor of an apartment building, and it is 2:00 a.m. in the dead of winter, paper training will seem like an absolutely splendid idea!

Paper training is convenient if I am a small dog but, if I am a large dog, it is impractical to expect me to urinate on paper unless you plan to paper the entire room. Over the long run it is better to train me to go outdoors. Sometimes, you can be successful in using a combination of outdoor and paper training. For example, outdoor training could be used during the day if someone is at home and paper training at night or vice versa. However, teach me one method at a time. To facilitate paper training when I am alone in the house, put my crate or bed in a confined area, leave the door of my crate open, and spread plenty of newspapers nearby.

There is **NO** valid argument for the use of hands to shake, swat, spank or wield a rolled up newspaper in housetraining or **ANY** other aspect of your relationship with me. **(The authors feel that rubbing a puppy's nose in its mistake is cruel. They believe that it does nothing except humiliate the puppy and lessen the bond between the puppy and its owner.)** If you catch me in the act, say "No" firmly. Pick me up when I have finished and take me outdoors to my designated potty area saying the word "potty" or whatever word you have chosen. If you discover an accident, after the fact, simply clean it up and disinfect the area with an odor neutralizer, such as a solution of one half water and one half white vinegar. Scolding me for having an accident will do no good since I am not able to associate my misdeed with the punishment. I want to please you, but it may take a while to figure out how. Remember it requires two to three years before most humans are out of diapers. So be patient and cut me some slack when I do not catch on right away. During the housetraining period, I need constant supervision. Therefore, do not let me have the run of the house. If you have questions or problems with housetraining, consult my veterinarian. I could have a medical disorder that requires attention.

Pet supply stores sell sprays, housetraining pads and other aids to be used on or near the door that I use when going outside. The products are intended to train me to use the same door each time I go out. I have heard that some puppies, like Nevi, take great delight in shredding the pads. Should this occur, eliminate the pads from the training process. It is best to confine me to tile or linoleum floors during the training period. If I stain a carpet or drapes, spray products are available to remove the odor and the stain. Do not use ammonia products because these smell like urine and will attract me back to the same area. If I am a male dog and have not learned that peeing into the wind is a mistake, there are sprays that can be used to clean my coat between baths. Crates can be an aid in housetraining. (See Paws to consider/SLEEPING, page 37.) Housetraining may take six to eight weeks or longer. I will have relapses in stressful situations such as scolding, having visitors or being in strange surroundings. Eventually, I may sit by the door or bark when I want to go outside. You will be ecstatic!

When walking with me, be sure to take your pooper scooper to clean up after me. In some cities, it's the law!

DON'T DO IT THERE!

I potty on the rug and someone points to my mistake;
A loud and angry voice can make a little puppy quake!

I cannot think in human terms or know the value of
The rugs and carpets in the room, possessions that you love.

I have a language of my own, as all my actions show;
My body language says it all, a "dog speak" you should know.

So when I must relieve myself, I whine or sniff the floor;
These signs should tell you to politely show me to the door.

And when we take our walks, don't let me leave my calling card,
In city parks and walkways, or worse yet, a neighbor's yard.

Just use a scoop and plastic bag; clean up my residue.
Be constant in your thoughtfulness; folks judge your dog by YOU!

THREE TO FOUR MONTHS

I weigh _____. I am _____ tall.

This month I've learned: _____

_____

I took my first walk at _____ months.

I walked to _____

My owner carried me for _____ blocks.

I learned to climb stairs at _____

I went down the stairs at _____. My method for

going down the stairs was _____

I followed _____ up or down the stairs.

I tore up the _____

My owner said, _____

I dug in the flower garden. Yes/No (circle one). When I did, my owner said, _____

_____

When the neighbors overheard, they said, _____

My owner did the following to prevent me from digging again: _____

_____

I had my first bath at _____ months, at the _____,

in the _____ or on the _____

I needed a bath because I _____

I liked it _____; I hated it _____; I gave my owner a bath

_____. Don't ever think of doing that to me again _____!

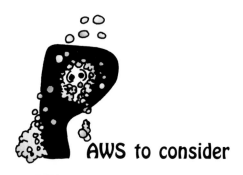

PAWS to consider

BATHING. The first rule when bathing me is never wear anything that says "dry clean only." As a puppy, bathe me only when needed. When I am an adult dog, I will need a bath two or three times a year. The exceptions are an encounter with a skunk, a strong doggy odor, dirt that cannot be removed with a brush, oily skin or after swimming in salt water. If doggy odor is a problem, moistened towelettes, sprays or baking soda keep my coat clean and fresh smelling between baths. When using baking soda, sprinkle it onto my fur, and rub it in with your hands. Wait five minutes, then brush it out. Other sprays are available to remove odor from carpets, upholstery, my bedding and the car.

Daily hair brushing keeps my skin and coat clean and healthy and eliminates the need for excessive bathing. Bathing me too often, especially before the age of six months, depletes my oil glands, causing itchy, dry skin. However, excessive itching may signal an allergy that requires medical attention. (See SOME DOGGONE GOOD ADVICE, page 135.) Give sponge baths with a quick rinse when I am young, and never wet bathe me before the age of two months or if I am ill.

Use quality bath products made for dogs, not humans. Do not use dish soap. Dog rinses are available for tangles and conditioning. Dry bath products are available for cleaning when using water is not practical. Medicated shampoos help soothe skin ailments and prevent parasitic accumulation. These shampoos should remain on the skin for several minutes, so read the instructions before using.

Most of us are not crazy about bathing, so assistance may be needed at first. You may need to use a leash to secure me to a nearby object so I will not bolt and run, leaving a soapy trail of water behind me. Before my bath, brush my coat removing surface debris and any matted hair. Placing two drops of mineral oil in each eye before bathing me or using no-tears shampoo will protect my eyes. My bathing area should not be slippery. The depth of the water should reach my knees, with the water temperature being warm, not hot or cold. Slowly introduce me to my bath. Lather me from my head back, taking care not to get lather in my eyes or water in my ears. Consult my veterinarian about the proper way to clean my ears and eyes. Wash my face with a sponge or soft cloth. Be sure to rinse me thoroughly. Shampoo left on my skin or hair can be very irritating and may cause a rash. Double-coated dogs like Nevi, an American Eskimo, are difficult to rinse. One-fourth cup of vinegar in one quart of water will help rinse out the soap.

Towel dry me thoroughly, gently drying my ears. Let me shake and then towel dry again. Blow dryers may frighten me, and unless set on the very coolest setting can burn my skin. If used, dryers should be held at least twelve inches from my skin and not be directed toward my eyes. In winter, keep me inside and away from drafts until I am completely dry. In very warm weather, I can dry outside, but I may roll in the dirt to rid myself of the shampoo smell. Brush me only when my hair is completely dry.

PHOTOS OF ME IN THE SUDS

YOUR HANDS

Your hands in daily grooming help my hair stay neat and clean;
Your hands, to bathe and brush me, give my coat a healthy sheen.

Your hands perform great wonders when accompanied by praise;
Your hands can work to build a bond of trust in many ways.

Your hands are used to teach me and to make my training fun;
Your hands can offer me a treat for every task well done.

Your hands can throw the ball that I will eagerly pursue;
Your hands in gentle stroking say, all good things come from you.

Your hands say, "Hi, how are you?" when you greet me after work;
Your hands will give me loving care when I am sick or hurt.

Your hands are used with lots of love, but not to spank or shake;
Your hands will be a blessing so our bond of trust won't break!

PHOTOS OF HANDS CARING FOR ME

48

aws to consider

GROOMING. Taking care of me requires about fifteen minutes a day, and you and I deserve this fifteen minutes together. Grooming creates a special bond between us and is essential for my health. Hair that is not brushed regularly can mat. Removing knots of matted hair is painful for me.

Purchase good quality grooming equipment. A long-haired dog will need a wire brush or natural bristle brush. A short-haired dog will need a hound glove (a mitt with short bristles in the palm), a metal comb or curry brush. Consult my veterinarian or a pet supply store for the proper grooming tools for me. Accustom me to being handled before starting the grooming process. Stroke my hair, touching my ears, mouth and feet. I may be sensitive about having my feet touched so take that part slowly.

Grooming should consist of the following:

HAIR/SKIN. Daily brushing is necessary for a long-haired dog, and brushing two or three times a week should be sufficient, for a short-haired dog. Start with short grooming sessions, brushing small areas each time until I become accustomed to brushing. When brushing do not yank my hair; instead, hold my skin gently with one hand and carefully brush in the direction required for my breed. After brushing, gently comb through my hair. If there are mats that cannot be combed out, work the comb under the mats. Then lift the mats away from my skin and carefully cut them out using blunt-nosed scissors. Bathing me makes hair mats worse since water tightens the knots. My skin is a good barometer of my general health, so check it for irritation or lumps while brushing me. A short-haired dog that spends lots of time in the sun may need to have suntan lotion rubbed into its skin. Use unscented SPF15 hypo-allergenic suntan lotion. If I suffer sunburn, take me to my veterinarian. Before having my hair clipped for the summer months, consult my veterinarian. It is not advisable for some breeds.

Petroleum jelly applied generously to burrs makes them easier to remove. Chewing gum can be removed from my hair by rubbing peanut butter on the gum. Wait five minutes and then try combing the gum gently out of my hair. Do not use any solvents that might burn my skin. It is generally easier to use blunt-nosed scissors to cut gum, paint or tar from my hair.

EARS. My ears should be inspected once a week for redness, swelling or excessive ear wax. Lift each ear flap and sniff the ear canal. A foul odor may be a symptom of infection. If you suspect problems, contact my veterinarian. Clip hair that might block air from entering my ears. A flop-eared dog may be prone to ear infection due to air blockage and the hair inside the ear may need to be removed. Excessive ear wax can be removed by cleaning my ears gently with cotton balls dipped in white vinegar or canine ear cleaning solution. Do not use soap and water. Always dry my ears thoroughly after cleaning, taking care not to let moisture accumulate. Never probe into my ears.

EYES. Check my eyes once a week. They should be bright and clear with no red spots around the iris. Rubbing my eyes against furniture or on the floor may indicate I have an eye problem or an allergy. If there is excessive discharge from my eyes, use a soft clean cloth or cotton ball soaked in boric acid or warm water to remove the discharge. Wipe gently under my eye moving outward from the inside corner. A white dog like Nevi may be susceptible to stains under the eyes from tearing. Medications are available from the veterinarian that, when added to food, reduce the discoloration. To keep the discharge from soaking into the coat, some breeders suggest using a small amount of zinc oxide ointment below the inside corner of the eye. Be careful not to get any of the ointment into the eye. Excessive eye discharge should be checked by my veterinarian. Salves are available to sooth hunting dogs' eyes that have been scratched by bushes or briars.

NOSE. My nose should be checked once a week for dryness, excessive discharge or sunburn. Dryness and discharge can be signs of infection. A foul odor from my nose, swelling or difficulty breathing may be a sign of sinus infection, tumor or the presence of a foreign object. Check with my veterinarian when any of these conditions exist. Some outdoor dogs may need sun protection on their noses.

FEET. Inspect my foot pads regularly for foreign objects, such as thorns, and for cracks. Canine foot moisturizer is available for cracked dry foot pads. Trimming the hair from between the footpads of long-haired breeds helps keep materials, such as mud, from accumulating there. Use blunt-nosed scissors.

Grooming reduces parasites, maintains a healthy coat and skin, and distributes my natural oils. Dry dermatitis, which causes hair loss and dry, scaly skin can be caused by a lack of grooming. Other causes are poor nutrition, excessive bathing, overheated rooms, insect bites, allergies, stress, staphylococcus bacteria or hormonal imbalance. If I develop dermatitis, my veterinarian can diagnose the problem and recommend treatment or change in my lifestyle. Consult my veterinarian or breeder for a demonstration of proper grooming. For the first month, keep the grooming sessions short.

If grooming is not your cup of tea, find a groomer you like and one who likes dogs, and begin to take me for grooming at an early age. Make sure the groomer maintains a clean and secure facility. A reputable groomer will require proof of inoculations prior to grooming me and will provide references. Do not use a groomer who suggests tranquilizing me before grooming. Some groomers are willing to make house calls.

MORE PAWS

PETicures. This is an intimidating project, and I will do everything possible to further your intimidation because I would rather make friends with the neighborhood cat than have my toenails cut. I will wiggle, whine, bite, cry and give you the dirtiest looks you have ever seen! If I would cooperate, the toenail clipping would take approximately two minutes. It has been known to take weeks, once you lose control.

Ask my veterinarian to demonstrate nail clipping. If nail clipping is not for you, take me to the veterinarian or groomer for this task. Should you decide to tackle nail clipping, do not wait too long because my over-grown nails may cause foot problems. Check with my veterinarian to see if I have dewclaws, located on the inside of each leg, that must be trimmed. They can curl and grow inward causing lameness.

Before cutting my toenails, gather all nail trimming supplies. You will need nail clippers designed for dogs. You may also need a clean white cloth, styptic powder or a flour and water paste in case you accidentally cut the vein in my nail. Lay me on my side, and give me something terrific to chew, like a pig's ear. This is similar to the "silver bullet theory," and it works! While I am occupied, grasp my foot, but not so firmly that I feel too restrained. It is better to trim my nails more often than cut too much of the nail at once, since you may cut the vein, which provides blood to the nail. If you should accidentally cut the vein, do not panic. The bleeding will not last long. Apply pressure, a small amount of styptic powder or the flour and water paste to the end of my nail to stop the bleeding. Give me plenty of love, and promise never to do it again! I will forgive you and promptly forget it. However, at this point it would be better to discontinue the trimming until another day. If I have dark nails, it is often difficult to see the veins. Therefore, you may want my veterinarian or groomer to trim my nails.

Check my paws occasionally for cuts or for small sharp objects that may have penetrated them. Limping or excessive licking of my paws may indicate that I have a problem. When a superficial wound is found, wash the area with warm water and apply an antiseptic. For a deep wound, take me to my veterinarian. Remove any sharp objects from my paws and treat in a similar manner. In case a fishhook is imbedded in my paw, take me to my veterinarian to have it removed. If I should suddenly react negatively when I have become accustomed to nail clipping, check my paws for a problem, such as an infection, a cracked nail or embedded foreign object. When a problem is beyond your expertise, call my veterinarian.

FURTHER PAWS

DENTAL HYGIENE. I go through two teething periods as a puppy. The first begins at sixteen weeks when my permanent teeth start to emerge. The other begins at eight months when my molars cut through the gums. If my baby teeth do not come out naturally by six months of age, they <u>must</u> be extracted by my <u>veterinarian</u>.

My need to chew becomes incessant during my teething period. Give me items that are safe to chew. If you do not want me to chew on your good shoes, then do not allow me to chew on your old shoes! Unfortunately, I have not been endowed with deductive reasoning and cannot distinguish the old from the new. Allowing me to chew on your fingers while teething or at other times may cause me to become a biter as I grow older. (See PAWS to consider/CHEWING, page 59.)

Feeding me soft foods and table scraps will cause me to develop tartar buildup earlier than if I am fed a balanced dry canine diet. The dry food aids in scraping the teeth so tartar cannot form. A tartar control food is now available for adult dogs. You can prevent tartar buildup at the gumline by brushing my teeth with a canine toothpaste and a canine toothbrush (Nevi's method). Human toothpaste or baking soda can cause gastric problems. Finger toothbrushes, oral solutions, cleaning pads (Chip's method), and breath sprays are also available. Before using any canine dental products, read the product instructions. Chew toys, dog biscuits, beef hide treats and dry food also help to clean my teeth. Take note that some basted beef hide treats can stain carpeting.

To introduce me to tooth brushing, spread a little canine toothpaste on my toothbrush and let me lick it. Gradually introduce the brush to the inside of my mouth. Gently lift my lip and brush a few teeth, or brush one side of my mouth one day and the other the next. Use a circular or back and forth motion. The outside surfaces of my teeth need the most attention and are the easiest to reach. When you have finished, give me lots of praise and love.

My dental care should start early. If this was not possible and you suspect periodontal disease, take me to my veterinarian for a check up. Signs of periodontal disease include:

- Tartar buildup and the presence of pus
- Discolored teeth
- Swollen, red, inflamed, sore or softened gum tissue
- Head shaking
- Loose or missing teeth
- Loss of appetite
- Bad breath

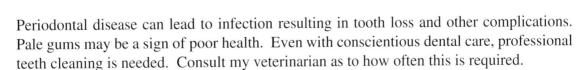

Periodontal disease can lead to infection resulting in tooth loss and other complications. Pale gums may be a sign of poor health. Even with conscientious dental care, professional teeth cleaning is needed. Consult my veterinarian as to how often this is required.

52

THE IZE HAVE IT!

They verbalize our exploits 'til the tales are over-sized.
They think we're more than just their dogs.... We're people in disguise!

They dress us up in clothes and boots! What can their brains devise?
'Til we resemble human-folk; we're just a different size!

We're fanticized, romaticized; We're publicized and idolized;
We're energized, and emphasized. We've even been mythologized!

Deodorized, not mongrelized! It comes as no surprise.
We're maximized and scrutinized, their single enterprise!

If they could learn to empathize with wisdom of the wise,
They'd let us live our lives as dogs. Now <u>that</u> is paradise!!!

PHOTOS OF ME LOOKING MY BEST

PAWS to consider

EXTERNAL PARASITES. The most common external parasites that plague me are fleas, ticks and mites. These feed on my blood while living on my skin and inside my ears. Cleaning my bedding often and brushing my coat regularly will minimize parasitic infestations.

FLEAS. Fleas can cause anemia and, in rare cases, death. They can transmit tapeworm and cause severe flea allergy dermatitis. Excessive scratching or biting myself, or exhibiting bald spots or scabby sores may be signs that I have fleas. Fleas can be seen with the naked eye. Flea dirt (dried blood pellets) may be found in my hair. When flea dirt is placed on a wet, white paper towel, it turns red. Flea dirt resembles ground pepper.

To get rid of these tenacious pests you should quickly and aggressively battle them on four fronts: our <u>home</u>, <u>yard</u>, my <u>bedding</u> and <u>me</u>. Consult my veterinarian for effective products. To maximize the flea kill, thoroughly vacuum all carpets and rugs, throwing away the vacuum bag. Treat our home and my outside area with an insecticide. If the flea infestation is severe, contact a professional extermination service. Bathe me with a good flea control shampoo. Make a thick lather around my neck to prevent fleas from running into my ears or nose. Fleas in these areas are much harder to treat. If I need further treatment, take me to my veterinarian or groomer for a flea dip. Sprays and powders are available for use between baths, but use only one product at a time unless approved by my veterinarian. Always take care not to get any product in my eyes. Read the product instructions carefully before using. Cedar chips inside my pillow bed are effective against fleas.

If you intend to purchase a flea collar for me, be aware of the following precautions:

- Do not use flea collars on me before the age of three months.
- Check under my collar frequently for an allergic reaction.
- Let the flea collar air out for twenty-four hours before using it the first time.
- Do not keep a flea collar on me when I go to bed or am in an enclosed space, such as a car. The fumes from the collar can be harmful.
- Never let me chew on my flea collar since it is toxic.

Oral or topical flea control product can be prescribed by my veterinarian. The authors prefer a prescription method of flea control called PROGRAM®. Chip and Nevi are given one tablet each month with food. If a female flea bites either dog, the flea ingests an ingredient that is passed to her eggs. The ingredient inhibits the life cycle of the flea by preventing her eggs from hatching. The female can lay from twenty-five to fifty eggs a day. PROGRAM® does not kill adult fleas. Therefore, it may be necessary to temporaily use conventional flea products with PROGRAM®, if you already have an infestation. Starting PROGRAM® in advance of the flea season will prevent an infestation. Give PROGRAM® year round in warm climates. PROGRAM® is safe for pregnant dogs and for puppies that are six weeks or older. It is harmless to the environment because it is not an insecticide.

LICE. Lice may be difficult to see. Sometimes the nits (eggs that the female lays on the hair shaft) can be seen. If you cannot find visible evidence for why I am scratching and biting continuously, lice may be the problem. A severe infestation of lice can leave me weak from blood loss. The treatment for lice is similar to flea treatment. Consult my veterinarian about the use of powders, dips or insecticide sprays.

MITES. Mites are transmitted to me from other infested animals. Mites, which are barely visible, can cause mange, skin lesions, infections and even death. Ear mites are responsible for serious ear infections and when present cause me to excessively scratch my ears. I may cry and squeal when I scratch. The discomfort may cause me to tilt my head to one side when walking. If you notice sores around my ears or a foul smell in my ear canal, the problem could be ear mites. Nasal mites may be present if there is an excessive discharge from my nose. Mites may be transmitted to humans. Consult my veterinarian if you suspect mites.

RINGWORM. Ringworm is a fungus, not a worm. It is most common in puppies but can be contracted by older dogs. Symptoms of ringworm are loss of hair in the infected areas and patches of dry, scaly skin that continue to enlarge as the disease spreads. Ringworm is contagious to animals and humans. Consult my veterinarian for treatment.

TICKS. Ticks are responsible for severe infections such as Rocky Mountain Spotted Fever and Lyme disease. The tick which causes Lyme disease is so small that it is difficult to see. If I am at risk for Lyme disease, ask my veterinarian about the Lyme vaccine. The clinical symptoms for Rocky Mountain Spotted Fever are high fever, decreased appetite, depression, enlarged lymph nodes, dehydration, weight loss, possible swelling of the legs and lower abdomen, and hemorrhaging from tissues of the mouth. The clinical symptoms of Lyme disease are lethargy, fever, depression, arthritis, sudden onset of severe pain, lameness or loss of appetite. If I exhibit any of these symptoms, take me to my veterinarian immediately. In warm weather please check me often for ticks, including my ear flaps and between my toes.

When a tick is found, you will need to remove it. Canine-safe tick insecticides can be applied directly to the tick. They kill the tick, causing it to release its hold on me. Another effective tick removal method is the use of tweezers. Hold the tweezers against the skin and remove the whole tick and destroy it. The tick's head is quite small and must be removed or it can cause an infection if left under my skin.

After removal, apply an antiseptic to the bite area. Should it be necessary to take me to the veterinarian, put the tick in a plastic bag and take it with you. A tick can infect you, too, so do not handle it with your bare hands. If we live in an area where ticks are numerous, clear my yard of weeds and tall grasses.

THE ITCH

We dogs, regardless of our breed,
Are set upon by parasites;
On us they simply love to feed,
Those pesky fleas and ticks and mites.

We claw and paw and scratch and bite;
The itch just makes us sassy.
We're not immune, so it's a plight,
For every lad and lassie.

So dust us with a pesticide,
From hackles to our fannies;
There'll be no place for pests to hide,
On Fidos, Scamps and Annies!

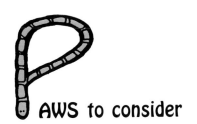

AWS to consider

INTERNAL PARASITES. The most common internal parasites are heartworm, round-worm, tapeworm, hookworm and whipworm. Most of these parasites live in my intestines, although the heartworm, in its adult stage, lives in my heart and blocks the blood flow. During my first year, I need to be tested often for internal parasites. As an adult dog, I should be tested once a year or if I exhibit symptoms. Scooting my bottom on the ground is generally not a symptom of worms but of impacted anal glands which require veterinary attention. Internal parasites should be treated by my veterinarian, since over-the-counter products are generally ineffective. Removing feces from my yard prevents reinfection.

HEARTWORM. Heartworm infestations are the most dangerous but, luckily, the most preventable. It is transmitted from an infected dog to me through mosquito bites. Unfortunately, symptoms may not present themselves until it is too late to save me. Symptoms of heartworm are coughing and extreme weakness. On my first visit to my veterinarian, which is about eight weeks of age, I will receive the heartworm preventative. The preventative can be given in liquid form or chewable daily or monthly tablets. It is usually given year round. At my yearly veterinary visit, my blood sample will be checked for evidence of heartworm. If it tests negative, I will continue my regular heartworm dosage. Treatment options will be discussed if evidence of heartworm is present. I will need to be tested yearly.

HOOKWORM. Hookworm can cause anemia and severe intestinal problems. I can contract hookworm when I come in contact with the fecal material of another dog. Hookworm may cause me to vomit, have black tarry stools or be lethargic.

ROUNDWORM. Roundworms can be seen in my feces. They resemble pieces of spaghetti and can be passed to me from my mother. I should be tested at my first visit to my veterinarian and thereafter, as often as my veterinarian recommends. Signs of roundworm are worms or mucus in the feces, diarrhea, a dull coat or a potbellied appearance.

TAPEWORM. Tapeworms live and consume digested food in my intestines. I contract them by eating infected fleas, rodents or rabbits. Check my stool and around the anus for white rice-like segments.

WHIPWORM. Whipworms live in my large intestine. I may have no symptoms, or I may develop diarrhea, dehydration or weight loss. Whipworms are found throughout the United States and are difficult to eradicate. I contract them by eating feces containing whipworm eggs.

Remove fecal material frequently from my yard. The ground in my yard may contain whipworm, roundworm or hookworm larvae from the fecal material of an infected dog. If I sleep in the grass, the larvae can work their way into my foot pads and then migrate to my intestines. With the exception of heartworm, worms can be detected by a fecal exam.

PUPpourri

I have had the following parasites: _____

_____

My doctor gave me _____

I took my medicine in my _____, on my _____,

with a _____, stuffed inside a _____

I spit it out (yes/no), swallowed it whole (yes/no), clamped my mouth shut (yes/no), never

noticed it (yes/no).

My favorite activities to do with my owner are _____

_____

My favorite toys are _____

I can carry _____ in my mouth.

I like to bury my toys and bones _____

I amuse myself by _____

_____

I respond to loud noises by _____

When my owner comes home, I greet him/her by _____

My owner greets me by _____

When I meet another dog, I _____

When I meet a cat, I _____

Things I like to chew are _____

I was in big trouble when I chewed _____

PAWS to consider

CHEWING. Chewing is essential for me. It provides comfort, maintenance of teeth and assistance in the cutting of molars. It also controls tartar, strengthens jaw muscles, and relieves boredom. I will need an ample supply of safe chew toys and treats to satisfy my need to chew. I sometimes engage in destructive chewing when I am bored. (See PAWS to consider/ BEHAVIORAL PROBLEMS, Page 106.) My options are limited. I cannot turn on the television, lose myself in a good book, or pick up the phone and invite a friend over. So I engage in chewing anything that will fit between my jaws. I also chew to relieve anger. Believe it or not, sometimes when we puppies resort to destructive chewing, it is because we love our owners and desperately want their attention. (In that case, Chip and Nevi must worship their owners! Chip chewed through a television cable and luckily did not receive a shocking jolt. He also made an unsightly mess of his owner's kitchen door molding. Nevi chewed and tore off the bottom half of a chair. His owner gave him too much freedom too soon and learned an expensive lesson. Both Chip and Nevi have "eaten" a dog pillow.)

If I engage in a destructive act, remember that it is you, my owner, who has made it possible for me to get into mischief. Vow to do a better job of supervising me and let bygones be bygones. When you catch me misbehaving, scold me and remove me from the area, giving me something acceptable to chew, such as a chew stick or hard toy. This is called positive training. Unless you discover me in a destructive act, it is useless to discipline me because I will not be able to relate my behavior to the punishment. If you come home from work and discover that I have shredded some of your possessions, please do not scold me. I will not understand the connection between the scolding and the chewing. Rather, I will relate the scolding to your return. Then I will begin to dread your arrival home since it will be unpleasant. I may even cower and hide each time you enter instead of greeting you joyfully. If you are worried that I will chew through the house while you are away, keep me in my crate or a confined area where I will not get into trouble. Leave safe chew toys or treats for me. Pet stores sell sprays that can be applied to my fur, furniture, doors or any other objects that I am inclined to chew.

Nylon chews come in flavors and are the safest. Chews should always be larger than my mouth, so they cannot be swallowed whole. I need supervision when chewing rawhide because I may choke on small pieces. Rawhide made in the United States is generally safer than foreign made rawhide which might contain harmful substances. The authors use ROAR-HIDE™ by Nylabone® Products which Chip and Nevi love. For more information about chew treats, talk to my veterinarian.

If I am constantly chewing because I am teething, try wetting a clean cloth, twisting it and freezing it. Let me chew it until it thaws; then repeat the process. The cold will numb my gums and chewing will aid the teething process.

PUPpourri

My most adorable habits are _____

_____

My most disgusting habits are _____

_____

PAWS to consider

DISGUSTING HABITS. Just because you dress me in a jogging suit and feed me from a silver bowl doesn't mean that I am not a dog. And, as such, I am capable of some disgusting acts. I may bring dead things to your attention or devour and then vomit them... usually in front of you. I may roll in the mud or another animal's stool, eat bugs and feces. In the winter I may like to toss frozen feces into the air and play with them. We puppies think "poopsicles" are fun.

However, playing can lead to eating, especially if I am bored. To curb this habit remove all feces from my yard frequently. There is a product called FOR-BID™ by ALPAR Laboratories that is available from my veterinarian. It should be given with my food morning and evening for five to six days. The bi-products of FOR-BID™ appear in my stool making it distateful to me. Ingesting feces regularly is not normal and may be a bad habit or the result of worms or a nutritional imbalance. Consult my veterinarian.

As far as my other "faux paws" are concerned, be patient and I will usually outgrow them. Always let me know by your tone of voice when you are unhappy with my behavior. Distract me to a new activity and clean up whatever I have left behind. (See PAWS to consider/BEHAVIORAL PROBLEMS, Page 106.)

I will get into trouble now and then no matter how closely I am watched. According to Brewer's Dictionary of Phrase and Fable, Sir Isaac Newton had a little dog named Diamond. One day Diamond knocked over a candle on Newton's desk. The candle flame set fire to papers on the desk and destroyed work that Newton had been researching for years. After Newton discovered the disaster, he lamented, "Oh, Diamond, Diamond! Thou little knowest the mischief thou hast done." Newton immediately set about reconstructing his work. Oh, that you all could be that patient!

PHOTOS OF ME DOING MY OWN THING

FOUR TO FIVE MONTHS

I weigh _____. I am _____ tall.

This month I've learned: _____

_____

I learned to jump on a sofa at _____ months.

I was immediately told _____

I visited the veterinarian on _____
(I need a check-up between four and five months)

I was checked for _____

I was given the following shots: _____

_____

My veterinarian said that I was _____

_____

My rabies license number is _____

Besides going to the vet, I like to ride to _____

with _____

because _____

I took my first trip to _____

I didn't get to go. My owner left me with _____ (I'm still too
young to stay at a kennel.)

My owner traveled to _____

My owner brought me a _____

My first camp out was at _____

My first hike was to _____

 AWS to consider

CAR SAFETY AND TRAVEL. Because I may become frightened by a car's motion, introduce me gradually to car travel by taking short trips. If I am prone to motion sickness, cover my area in the car. Motion sickness medication can be prescribed by my veterinarian. Sometimes honey will relieve my car sickness. It is not wise to take me for a ride shortly after I have eaten. Once I am comfortable with car travel, increase the travel time.

While riding in a car, I should be secured by a car restraint or a dog car seat. In California and Oregon it is the law! A car seat is usually used for a small dog, while a harness is used for a large dog. The harness has an opening that allows a car seat belt to pass through it and is very effective. This type of car restraint allows me to sit or lie down. The restraint prevents me from jumping onto your lap while you are driving and may keep me from being injured when you stop suddenly. It prevents me from jumping out of the window when I see something exciting like a rabbit or a fast food restaurant. We puppies can smell those hamburgers a mile away. Most puppies like to ride in a vehicle with their heads hanging out the window. There is nothing better than the exhilarating feeling of the wind in our hair and

ears while sniffing, in rapid succession, the luscious scents of mother nature. However, if I am allowed to hang my head out of the window, I could sustain an eye injury from particles that are thrown up by passing vehicles. Window guards are available that fit into the window areas. They are steel devices that allow fresh air in, but do not allow me to hang my head out of the window. Riding in a convertible with the top down can be very dangerous for me.

My crate can secure me when riding in the back of a pick-up or the back seat of a car. For long trips, the crate should contain food, water and a toy. The crate should be bolted to the pick-up and should not be placed in direct sunlight. There are tie-downs especially made for pick-up trucks. During the summer months I can suffer heatstroke or burn my paws from hot metal floors in a pick-up. During the winter I can suffer from frostbite, so please use extreme caution.

When taking me with you on vacation, walk me each morning before departing. Stop often during the trip to allow me fresh water, exercise and elimination. At rest stops, keep me on a leash in areas labeled "DOGS ONLY." It is best never to leave me in the car in very hot or cold weather since heat stroke or hypothermia can be life threatening. However, if you must leave me for a short time, roll the windows down a few inches, unfasten the seat belt from my restraint, leave water for me, and please hurry back. Consider this: A puppy is a prime target for theft if left alone in a car with the windows partially open. If you use window guards, they can be easily removed from the outside and do not keep me safe. It is against the law in Florida and Michigan to leave me alone in a car. At the end of each day's travel, feed me and take me for a walk.

64

When making travel plans, call the motel or campground to see if I am allowed in your room or campsite. If I am not, is there a kennel facility? If I am at your campsite, do not let me run loose. Bring a tie-out line to restrain me. Being restrained will protect me from the wildlife and vice versa. It will keep me from disturbing other campers. Remember to keep me away from the campfire and check me daily for parasites. When I am with you in a motel/hotel, be a considerate guest. Do not let me soil the carpet, bark excessively or destroy property. Use my crate to keep me out of mischief. I should not travel if I am ill or a female in heat and, ideally, not before the age of twelve weeks.

Before traveling, make sure all of my inoculations are up to date. Bring my health certificate showing my inoculations and general health status. This is important in case I need medical attention, am going to be boarded at a kennel, or am entering another country. Consult my veterinarian to see if the area to which I am traveling is an area where heartworm is prevalent. If I am not taking the heartworm preventative, start it four weeks before leaving and continue it after you return home. I will need a blood test before starting the preventative.

When traveling with me, consider packing some or all of the following, depending on your travel plans:

- health certificate
- grooming equipment
- food and water bowl, a supply of water, dog food and dog treats (It is best not to change my diet. Water can be changed gradually over the course of the trip, but beware of letting me drink stream water. Some streams harbor parasites. The water must be boiled or purified before consuming. Water purifiers can be purchased at sporting goods stores.)
- a few favorite toys and chews
- a towel for swimming or a quick rinse
- plastic bags and a scoop or paper towels to clean up after me
- a well-ventilated, collapsible wire crate or bed
- prescribed medications and motion sickness medicine, if it is needed
- a seat restraint
- a collar with license and identification tag (If you will be staying in one place, it is a good idea to attach a temporary tag to the collar showing your vacation address and phone number).
- a leash (a short one for potty stops and a longer one for hiking to give me more freedom)
- a photo of me in case I am lost
- flea powder
- bag balm ointment for sore paws
- equipment for removing ticks if camping or hiking
- 3% hydrogen peroxide or antibacterial ointment, gauze bandages, gauze dressing pads, adhesive tape and scissors
- a first aid book
- a canine life preserver if I will be in a boat.

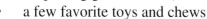

When traveling other than in a car, check with the carrier about its requirements for transporting animals. When traveling by air, a small dog can stay in the cabin, provided that it is confined in a dog carrier that fits under the seat. A reservation is needed. A large dog can be crated and put in the baggage compartment. An unaccompanied dog will be placed in the cargo area. Call passenger service for baggage travel and cargo service for cargo travel. Check-in for baggage service is at the passenger gate. Check-in for cargo service is usually at the air freight terminal. Call your carrier for the location. When traveling outside the continental United States, communicate well in advance with the Consulate of the country of destination for regulations regarding entry. The Consulate will generally be located in Washington D. C. Confirm travel arrangements with the airline twenty-four hours in advance.

If my travel involves changing planes from one airline to another, you will need to claim me after the first flight and check me in with the second airline. If there is time, I will appreciate exercise, a potty break, some water and lots of hugs. When changing planes within the same airline, I will be checked through by airline personnel. For long stop-overs, ask the airline personnel about my care or ask your travel agent about the availability of kennels at the airport.

You will need to bring my crate or rent one from the carrier. The carrier will require a health certificate for me that has been issued within ten days of the trip, identification tags for my crate and collar, and my plane ticket. The identification tags should include your name, home address and phone number, destination address and phone number and my name. The crate should be large enough for me to stand, turn around and stretch out on my side. The crate must be sturdy, easy to open and have nothing on it that can harm me. It must be <u>well</u> ventilated, and have 3/4" rims that prevent other shipments from blocking the air. You will need to indicate with arrows "This End Up" and the crate should be labeled with letters one inch high that read, "Live Animal or Animals." The crate must have handles so airline personnel can easily lift it. For long flights, food and water dishes should be secured to the inside of my crate. My food and my feeding schedule should be attached to the outside. Place absorbent bedding in the bottom of my crate.

Air travel is hard on dogs. I should not be shipped by air before the age of three months. Travel is not recommended for dogs that are ill, elderly, very young, pregnant or have breathing problems. Tranquilizers are usually not recommended because the effects at high altitudes are uncertain. A pug-nosed dog may have difficulty breathing during air travel. It is your responsibility to monitor my travel. The greatest danger to me is extremes in temperature inside and outside the aircraft. The plane's cargo section is not cooled or heated. Choose morning or evening flights during the summer since the weather will be cooler at those times. Schedule a non-stop flight for me. Six hours is considered the maximum time I should be kept in my crate. If I will be confined longer than six hours, consider another means of transportation. Check with my veterinarian before planning air travel.

Feed me a light meal well in advance of the trip. Exercise me before the trip. Withhold water one hour before the trip unless the weather is hot. In that case, give me a small amount of water. If I am traveling in my crate, do not use a choke collar or muzzle. These can cause me to strangle or suffocate.

A good source of information on pet travel is "Transportation Tips" from the Animal and Plant Health Inspection Service. Send a self-addressed, stamped envelope to APHIS, LPA/PI, 4700 River Road, Unit 51, Riverdale, MD 20737. "Travel Tips For You and Your Pet" can be obtained from The American Society for the Prevention of Cruelty to Animals by sending a self-addressed, stamped envelope to: ASPCA, Education Dept. 424 E. 92nd St. New York, NY 10128.

PHOTOS OF ME ON MY FIRST TRIP
OR ME AT MY FAVORITE HANG-OUT

68

 AWS to consider

BOARDING KENNELS. You may find it difficult the first time you have to leave me in the care of someone else. However, knowing that you have chosen a clean and safe facility for me should bring you peace of mind. A reputable boarding kennel should not accept me before the age of five months because I may not have had all of my inoculations or the full benefit of them. Before visiting kennels, obtain recommendations from friends or my veterinarian.

Here are some guidelines to consider when visiting a kennel and talking with the management:

- What is the kennel's philosophy about dog care? Does it agree with your own?
- Are the premises clean and dry? Is there a disagreeable odor permeating the facility?
- Are the stalls and fences in good condition?
- Does the kennel permit you to leave me for a few hours or for day care to prepare me for a two week stay? (This is nice, but don't discount the kennel if this service is not offered.)
- Does the kennel require proof of inoculations before accepting me?
- Does there seem to be a friendly relationship between the management and the staff?
- Does the kennel offer playtime for me daily or several times a week? (There is usually a charge for this service.)
- Are there concrete runs for exercise adjoining my stall?
- Are the staff gentle when handling me?
- Do the staff seem interested in me and do they make me feel at ease?
- Does the kennel have first aid kits, and are the staff knowledgeable enough to know if I need medical attention?
- Is the kennel bonded and insured?
- Is the kennel heated and air conditioned? Is there an alarm if the temperature rises or falls to a dangerous level?
- Is the kennel secure, and does it have a fire alarm?
- Is the stall large enough for me?
- Is my stall safe from other dogs? There should be a divider or wall between the stalls.
- Do the staff fill out forms concerning my needs, such as exercise, food, medications and veterinarian name? Do they allow you to bring my food from home?
- Is someone on duty at all times? If not, what arrangements are made for my safety?

Once you have chosen a boarding kennel, take the following with you when I will be boarded:

- Proof and dates of my inoculations.
- Medications if needed, with clear instructions for use.
- Complete food supply, if I have problems adjusting to a new diet.
- Safe chew toys, treats and biscuits and instructions on when to give them.
- Two rugs for sleeping. If one is soiled, a clean one can be put down. Make sure I cannot pull pieces off of the rug that could choke me if ingested.
- Veterinarian's name and phone number; and a number where you, a friend or relative can be reached.
- Any special instructions for me. (See DOG KENNEL CARDS at back of book.)
- Something of yours, like an old sock, that carries your scent to make me feel secure.

We puppies sometimes suffer from separation anxiety when we are away from our owners. To keep my feelings of separation from becoming severe, leave me at the kennel for a few hours or for day care once or twice before your trip. When I know that you will return, I will be better able to adjust. This reduces the likelihood of serious problems when you are away for a longer time. Before leaving me, check with the kennel about its dog pick up schedule.

There are other options to consider besides using a kennel. Friends or relatives may enjoy staying with me at their house or mine. If you decide to leave me with a friend, be sure the house and yard are safe and secure. If I am upset by your leaving, I may look for ways to escape and find you. Many cities have dog sitter services. Make sure the dog sitting service is insured, bonded and provides references. For a list of local sitters, call the National Association of Professional Pet Sitters (800-296-7387). The service will come to our home several times a day to feed, exercise and care for me. Use the dog sitter once before you leave on your trip. This will give you an opportunity to observe how the sitter treats me and it will give me time to become familiar with the sitter. Go with the sitter when I am walked to see how I am handled.

When you travel and leave me at home, confine me to a safe area where I cannot be destructive. Do not confine me to my crate since that would not allow me adequate exercise. Leave safe chew toys for me to entertain myself. If I have not been housetrained, surround my area with newspapers and keep me in a room with an easy to clean floor. Leave a generous stack of newspapers for the dog sitter and safe chew toys for me. Do not be surprised if I bypass the toys and tear up the newspapers because I am frustrated by your absence. Have the sitter come frequently enough for me to have ample opportunity to potty and to be given plenty of attention and exercise. Leave instructions for my care with the sitter. (See DOG SITTER CARDS at back of book.)

THE DOGGIE RAP

I am a people puppy, from my doggie point of view.
I've bonded with my people and we're stuck like super-glue!

We ride in their red pick-up truck; we wrestle in the grass;
Whenever we can hit the road, we always go first class!

We drive out to the countryside; our lunch is in a sack;
I'm going with my 'alpha dog,' the leader of my pack!

And when we're all together, I will never miss a trick,
To get my folks to play with me, to toss a ball or stick!

I'll race around and fetch 'em; and spend hours havin' fun;
I hate to give up later when my people say we're done!

I wear my leather jacket. It's one of my favorite duds.
It has an eagle on the back and lots of silver studs!

I have a zippered pocket for my many bones you see,
When we go joggin' all around, my people pack and me!

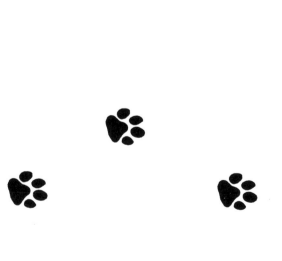

A STORY OR POEM ABOUT MY OWNER AND ME DOIN' FUN THINGS

_____

_____

_____

_____

_____

_____

_____

_____

_____

_____

_____

_____

_____

_____

_____

_____

_____

_____

72

PAWS to consider

TRAINING. The goal of a good training program is to help me become a well-behaved dog that is a credit to you. Through training, I should become willingly obedient.

Training is important for my safety and sociability. I suggest that you enroll the two of us in puppy school (sociability) when I am about four months old. I will not be ready for serious training (obedience school) until I am six months of age. Teaching me at home requires patience and a knowledge of dog training techniques. If you decide on home training, additional information is available through bookstores, libraries or dog training videos. If you plan to have me participate in dog shows, formal training is essential. Most communities provide a variety of classes that reflect various training methods and philosophies. Pick one that agrees with yours. It is a good idea to observe a training class at the school you are considering before enrolling me. Select a school that enforces positive training methods. I can be trained without using devices that cause pain. If I have a behavioral problem, such as barking excessively, digging, or biting, seek individual help from a dog trainer or a person who specializes in dog behavioral problems. Some will come to your home. (See PAWS to consider/BEHAVORIAL PROBLEMS, page 106.)

Schools require that you or a professional dog handler participate in all my lessons. To be effective, it is best that you take part in my training unless you are planning on adopting the trainer or having that person live-in. Usually only one person in my family will be allowed to take part in my training. However, all members of my family should be aware of the training methods and use the proper commands when interacting with me. Otherwise, I may not be responsive to them and they could undermine the work of my trainer. During training, it is a good idea to incorporate hand signals. This insures that if I become deaf in old age, I will still understand the command.

Classes at a training school usually last one hour, but you can start at home with short training periods of fifteen minutes or less. Wait two hours after I have eaten to begin a training session. Take me to a potty area before and after training. Have a supply of easy to eat doggy treats to reward me. Use a familiar setting or I may be distracted. After my lesson, spend a little time playing with me.

Always be positive! Copious amounts of patience and praise will assure my progress. If your patience wears thin, discontinue the lesson until you are composed. It may take several months to teach me to respond consistently to a command. Remember, that as a baby, you probably would have had difficulty with "heeling" and "staying" too. Be consistent and teach only one command at a time. State commands clearly in an authoritative manner, using my name first, followed by the command. Your voice is very important in my training. The tone should be decisive and commanding but not angry. If I do not respond to the command, make a correction, such as the word "No" or a quick tug on my leash. Never yell at me or strike me if it seems that I am not learning fast enough. Striking me does nothing except make me fearful and distrusting of you. When I am successful, give me lavish praise and a treat. Again, your voice is very important. Use a high pitched enthusiastic tone. When I am not successful, do not give a treat. Wait a few minutes, and then start the lesson again. If my training is not started until I am older, you may have to undo some negative learned behavior.

Four basic commands that I must learn are "come," "sit," "down" and "stay." For the sake of others, I must also learn the "off" command. Furthermore, it is important to learn the "no" and "heel" commands. The "stand" command is useful while grooming or at my veterinarian's office. The following are some simple directions to teach commands. These directions should not contradict my formal training, but if they do, follow the advice of my instructor. When training at home, teach the commands in the order presented because they follow a logical sequence. Continue to reinforce mastered commands as you move on to new ones.

<u>COME</u> At home, move some distance from me and, when I am distracted, say my name followed by the command, "come." Consistently use the same name in a cheerful tone of voice when calling me. When I come, give me a treat and generous praise. If I do not come, move closer. Let me see the treat, and then call me again. If I still do not come, continue to move closer using the "come" command. You should expect me to come <u>every</u> time I am called. I should associate coming to you as something pleasurable. Therefore, definitely use the "come" command at dinnertime, but when you must bathe me or clip my nails, you should come and get me. Never call me to you to reprimand me.

Use a long lead (at least twenty feet) during training outdoors. Keep me in an area with few distractions. Step away from me and then call me to you. If I do not come, gently pull me toward you and give me a treat. Gradually increase your distance from me. After I have mastered this command, go to a safe enclosed area and drop the lead. Move away from me and call me to you. When I come every time I am called, gradually discontinue the treats, but never the praise. If I break loose and start to run away, try this tactic. Do not chase me.

Instead, make lots of noise, call my name and run in the opposite direction. I will think it is a game and run after you. Then you can catch and praise me for coming to you.

SIT Place me in front and perpendicular to your body. Put one hand on the back of my collar. Lift my collar gently upward as you tuck my hind legs under me with your other hand. Never push down on my hindquarters since this may injure me. Say my name and the word "sit" as you position me. Keep me in the sitting position for five seconds; release and praise me. Select a release word such as "OK" or "Free." Continue the lesson for a few minutes each day until I sit on command. Once I have learned the command, keep me in the "sit" position for no more than one or two minutes.

DOWN Once I have learned to sit, half of the battle to learn to lie down is won. Place me in a sitting position. Place a treat near my nose, and lower the treat to the floor, saying my name and the command, "down." I should follow the treat to the floor and be in the "down" position. If this strategy fails to work after placing me in the sitting position, bend over or kneel at my left side facing the same direction I am facing. Put your right hand around me and behind my right foreleg. Put your left hand behind my left foreleg. Gently extend my legs forward and down into the "down" position. When I stay in the "down" position after you have released my legs, give me treats and praise. If, however, when you kneel beside me, I look up and cover your face with "kisses" don't be surprised. Be grateful and give me a big hug. Teach me "down" at a later time. For the time being, the kisses and hugs are more important.

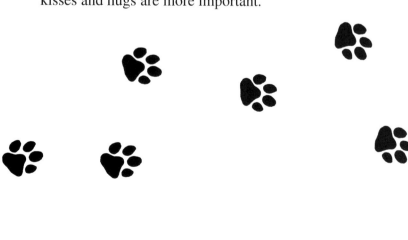

STAY Seat me at your left side with the leash attached to my collar. Hold the leash in your right hand keeping it loose. Pass your left palm in front of my face saying my name and the command, "stay." Step in front of me, starting with your right foot. Once in front of me, turn to face me and repeat the "stay" command. Try to keep me in the "stay" position for fifteen seconds. Then step back beside me and release me using the words "Ok" or "Free." Reward me with praise and treats. Repeat for a few minutes each day until I have mastered the "stay" for fifteen seconds.

Once this maneuver is accomplished, again step in front of me, using the right foot. Keep the leash loose. Face me and then take a few steps backward. At first you will not get very far before I try to join you. Each time I get up, hold your hand up, palm facing me and say, "No! Stay." Then put me back in the sitting position. After a few minutes, step beside me and release me. Each day continue practicing to increase the distance until you reach the end of my leash. Once I have learned this maneuver, try dropping the leash in a straight line in front of you, again using my name and the "stay" command. Continue to practice until I stay even though I am not on a leash. The "stay" is a very useful command and could possibly save my life some day. Eventually, teach me to stay when I am standing or lying down.

NO When teaching the "no" command, you must be firm and consistent. If you say "no" to something one day but not the next, you will confuse me. Say, "No!" in a firm voice when you see me doing something I should not be doing. I must learn that "no" means that I must immediately stop whatever I am doing and look to you for direction. If you do not get my attention, shout the word "No!" followed by my name. We puppies usually do not like loud noises and will respond. When I respond, praise me. Once I understand the command, saying "no" in an authoritative voice will be sufficient.

Remember, you are essentially dealing with a baby, so don't be too harsh and say "no" to everything I do. We puppies like to investigate and, as long as it is safe, let me have some fun. Sometimes I may become mischievous to get your attention, so stop and give me a few pats, a kind word or, better yet, some playtime.

HEEL A choke collar and a leash are used when teaching me to "heel." Start this training when I am old enough to use a choke collar, which is at six months of age or older. My authors feel that pinch collars should not be used under any circumstances.

Familiarize yourself with the following restrictions, before you attempt to use a choke collar:

- Never use a choke collar during training without proper instructions from the manufacturer or your dog trainer.
- Never use a choke collar when I am under the age of six months.
- Never allow me to wear my choke collar when I am confined to my crate or unattended.
- Never use a choke collar other than during my training sessions.

To begin the "heel" lesson, attach the leash to my choke collar and hold the loop at the end of the leash with your right hand. Gather most of the leash in your right hand, leaving some slack in the leash to be held loosely by the left hand. The left hand is used for corrections. With me sitting at your left side, begin walking with your left foot, saying my name and the command "heel." Walk briskly and in a straight line to hold my attention. My shoulder should be in line with your legs. As you walk, make firm, but gentle, short tugs on the lead to keep me aligned with your body. Use the "heel" command each time you step on your left foot. At first, I may be successful for ten to twenty seconds or a few steps. Always give me plenty of encouragement and praise. If I appear to be afraid or am falling behind, coax me into position. When I am forging ahead, slow your pace and make a couple of short, quick tugs on the leash. After the command is learned, use "heel" only when I forget. Each time you stop, I should immediately stop and sit by your left side. When I do not sit, use the method for the "sit" command. Just before stopping, say my name followed by the words, "Halt. Sit!" Always stop on your left foot. Once you have stopped walking and I am seated, use the release word. Praise me whether I am sucessful or not.

Once I have learned to "heel" walking in a straight line pattern, you can begin to vary the pattern. Start with wide turns to the left. Once I am successful try right-hand turns. After I have learned right-hand turns, repeat both the left and right-hand turns, making the turning area tighter. Don't be discouraged. It may take about two years to teach me to "heel" effectively.

If I become easily distracted during training, try the following procedure. Using a choke collar and at least a twenty foot lead, stand in one spot and let me wander away from you. When I am not looking at you, walk briskly in the opposite direction. When I feel the tug on the lead, I will look at you and follow. Walk a short distance; then stop and repeat the procedure. Practice each day until I understand that I must watch <u>you</u> to find out where I am going.

Once I am used to the idea of looking to you for directions, heeling will be much easier to teach. Heeling is taught for safety and for competing in dog shows. When we go out for a casual walk, it is not necessary for me to "heel" all the time. Our time together should be relaxed, and I should have time to explore.

<u>**OFF**</u> Believe it or not, some people will not consider me as wonderful as you do. They will be very unreceptive when I jump on them. Therefore, I must be taught the "off" command. If I am small and try to jump on you, quickly step backwards so I have nothing to jump on. I will find myself back on the floor in front of you. Say the command "off" as I return to the floor. Then praise me. If I am a large dog, quickly raise your knee to my chest, and with your hands, grasp my fore legs, pushing me away. Sternly say, "Off!" The idea is to form a barrier between us without hurting me. Use the "off" command when I jump up on the furniture. Be consistent with the "off" command, and insist that everyone in the family agrees on what I am allowed to do. Praise me when I obey. Once I have stopped jumping on people, allow me to greet visitors. When someone arrives, ask permission to allow me to greet them. If the guest agrees, take a few seconds and let us become acquainted. I will be satisfied and probably go on to something else.

STAND The stand command is very helpful when visiting the veterinarian or groomer. Place me in a sitting position. Take the leash in your right hand, and place your left hand under my belly in front of my hind legs. Pull the leash up and forward saying my name followed by the command, "stand." As I rise to stand, keep me from moving forward with your left hand. Wait for fifteen seconds, then release and praise me. If I do not catch on, manually place me in the standing position using my name and the stand command as you do it. Praise me even if I immediately sit down.

When I have mastered all the commands, try practicing with me off leash in a quiet, enclosed area. The above guidelines have shown you how to expect and get the best from me during training. For more concentrated learning, take me to a dog training school.

For puppy school you will need my health record, a leash, soft collar and plenty of treats that can be eaten quickly. Obedience school will require a health record, leash and choke collar. Contact the school regarding additional supplies.

(Chip's puppy school presented an excellent no-nonsense approach to positive teaching. Each participating puppy was required to perform specific functions regardless of distractions. Chip possessed an uncanny ability to unintentionally yet consistently be a distraction. As owners walked their puppies on leashes in the training arena, Chip managed to plant, without increasing or slowing his pace, a wet, slimy "kiss" indiscriminately on the passing puppies. While many of the puppies would have liked to respond to Chip's ardent advances, their serious minded owners kept them on the straight and narrow path. Each puppy, with guidance from owners and teachers, successfully completed the training course in spite of Chip's chummy connections.

At the final lesson of Nevi's puppy school, "graduation" took place. Each puppy was tested on what it had learned. Each was given a ribbon and/or a certificate. Nevi is very smart and probably would have finished first in his class, but Nevi is also "Mr. Congeniality." Therefore, during the final judging, even though he knew his lessons quite well, he thought it was much more important to take a detour and meet a lovely poodle that he had not met before. He was probably right. She turned out to be very nice. And from Nevi's point of view, what good was a ribbon? You can't eat it or play with it.)

NOTES ON MY TRAINING

_____

_____

_____

_____

_____

_____

_____

_____

_____

_____

_____

_____

_____

_____

_____

_____

_____

_____

PUPpourri

SCHOOL DAYS.

I started puppy school on _____

The name of my school is _____

My teacher's name is _____

I learn faster, slower or about the same as every other puppy in my class _____

I like puppy school because _____

_____

I have learned the following commands:

	Yes	No	I'm still working on it.
Come	____	____	____
Sit	____	____	____
Down	____	____	____
Stay	____	____	____
No	____	____	____
Off	____	____	____
Stand	____	____	____

My owner has learned to do the following: _____

_____

The command I know best is _____

I get a treat when I _____

My antics that make my owner laugh (in spite of my teacher's efforts to keep us serious) are

_____

The cutest thing I do is _____

MY SCHOOL PHOTO

MY GRADUATION CERTIFICATE

FIVE TO SIX MONTHS

I weigh _____. I am _____ tall.

This month I've learned: _____

_____

_____

I was housetrained by _____ months. The first time I barked to go outside

was at _____ months.

I lifted my leg to potty at _____
(This can be much later; both males and females squat at first)

I caught a ball at _____ months; a frisbee at _____ months.

I can also catch a _____

I can jump over _____

I can crawl under _____

My favorite places to take a walk are _____

I walk with _____

My favorite pet playmate's name is _____

My favorite pet playmate is a _____

My favorite place to play is _____

My favorite things to play with are _____

I like to play _____ with _____

I went swimming at _____ when I was _____ months old

with _____

I loved the experience, hated the experience, or was horrified that I did it. (circle one)

PHOTOS OF ME AT PLAY

EXERCISE. We puppies are lucky. We don't worry about our inner thighs, our bustlines or our sagging bottoms. If fed and exercised properly, we should never have a weight problem. But a steady stream of table scraps and lying on the couch watching old Lassie movies will put us at the same risk as humans. Fat puppies are uncomfortable and definitely unhealthy. Excessive weight can cause heart, digestive, respiratory and hip problems. If you think that I have developed a weight problem, consult my veterinarian about diet changes and exercise.

I need at least twenty minutes of vigorous exercise a day. Exercise will continue to build a bond between us, relax me, help to keep me from destructive behavior and make me healthier. Some breeds like retrievers and pointers need more exercise than others. Before embarking on an exercise program, consult my veterinarian about my general health and appropriate exercise. If I have not been exercised for awhile or am overweight, start out gradually, so I will not sustain injuries. Exercise in the coolest part of the day. Just because you put me outside, does not mean that I am getting exercise. If you do not want to participate in my exercise, sit in the backyard and toss a ball or stick for me to retrieve. If you choose to exercise with me, all the better. It will benefit both of us. Consider playing with a frisbee or ball, swimming or walking. My bones and muscles need a chance to develop properly before joining you in vigorous exercise, such as jogging or speed walking. Some breeds can develop hip problems if they are encouraged to jump at too early an age. Do not attach my leash to your bike and expect me to run along beside it. While trying to keep up with you, I can collapse or my footpads can be worn raw.

I will need my collar and leash when going for a walk. A nylon or soft leather collar is best when I am a puppy. Consider using reflective tape on my leash when walking me at night. Give me time to adjust to my collar before introducing a leash. At first I may fuss and scratch at my collar, but I will soon get used to it. Do not use a choke collar until I am at least six months old. A choke collar can injure my trachea before that age. After I am accustomed to my collar, attach my leash to it. At first, let me play with the leash so I will not be afraid of it. When I adjust to the leash, try taking me for a short walk.

In the beginning, walking with me may be difficult. I have a whole world to investigate, and I will probably walk every way but straight. If I wander, gently guide me back to where you want me. Jerking on my leash can injure me. As I become accustomed to our walks, I will walk beside you (some of the time). In the meantime, enjoy my curiosity and the additional exercise that I am providing for you, but watch for broken glass, sharp objects or small pebbles that could injure my paws. Take a scoop and plastic bag along to clean up after me. In some cities it's the law. When I am six months or older, you can begin to teach me to heel. (See PAWS to consider/TRAINING, page 76.)

Avoid exercising me in very hot, humid weather since I could suffer from heatstroke. If the pavement is too hot for you to walk across barefoot, then it is too hot for my little tootsies. Carry me over it so I will not damage my footpads. If my legs are short, the heat from the pavement on my belly will be very uncomfortable. When walking, carry enough water for both of us. Don't let me eat snow, drink from street puddles or melted snow, since they can contain toxic chemicals. After walking in wooded areas, check my coat and skin for burrs, ticks or thorns. Some cities have dog walking services if, for some reason, you cannot adequately exercise me.

During the winter, if we encounter de-icing compounds, wash my feet on arriving home. Remove snow or ice clumps from my footpads. If my foot pads are dry or cracked, apply canine moisturizer to them. Also, in very cold weather I can suffer frostbite. The ears, tail, scrotum and feet are most often affected. The symptoms of frostbite are reddened, white or grayish skin and sometimes shock. A short-haired or single-coated dog may need a sweater or coat before walking outside in the winter. Always dry me thoroughly after playing in the snow.

(Chip and Nevi regularly walk with their "parents" and seem very unhappy and restless when they miss their daily exercise. Nevi's "parents" sometimes walk fifteen miles in a weekend. Nevi goes with them and walks thirty miles since he never walks in a straight line. He is "ADVENTURE DOG" and, as such, loves to investigate and meet the world with a big smile on his face. When he was four months old, his inquisitiveness got him into trouble. He was in a fenced area so he was off his leash. He saw some ducks on a pond and immediately jumped in and paddled out to get a closer look. It suddenly dawned on him that he was no longer on solid ground. It was the middle of a typical Illinois winter, so no one wanted to go in after him. With a lot of coaxing and calling from his "parents", he paddled his little feet as hard as he could and made it to the edge of the pond. He was very happy to settle into some warm arms and be carried home. He hasn't been swimming since.

Chip is a Chocolate Labrador and, therefore, born to love water. Right? Wrong! During the summer Chip's "parents" tried coaxing, cajoling, even offering tasty treats to entice Chip into the lake for a swim. Their efforts were to no avail. Chip lay, with front paws dangling over the edge of the boat dock and a worried look on his face, refusing to enter the water. Two family friends appeared with their dogs, and the group began to wade into the lake. The dogs splashed, dived and retrieved tennis balls as Chip watched from a safe distance. Chip watched the four for nearly an hour. Then he hesitantly waded in from the shore. After several timid ventures into the water, he began to romp on shore with the other dogs. By the end of the day, even Chip was jumping from the dock and loving the water he was born to enjoy!)

H_2O K9

I have a thirst for summer fun that I would like to slake,
In ocean, river, swimming hole, perhaps a stream or lake.

The cool, refreshing water makes a puppy feel just fine,
It comes so very naturally to an **H_2O K9.**

So lock the house and say that we are going to the shore,
There, I can join a special group, the canine water corps.

Some dogs are boating, others sailing; some can surf or ski,
While many take a flying leap and dive and swim like me.

Just lead me to the water, summer fun that I adore,
A wet, full-blooded member of the canine water corps!

PHOTOS OF ME EXERCISING

LAWS to consider

LOST PUPPIES. I know that you take exceptionally good care of me. However, out of curiosity I may dig under a fence, or walk through a gate that is accidentally left open, or dash off on an adventure if my leash breaks. From what I have heard, it seems to be very difficult to find a lost puppy. Therefore, it is important that I have **some form of identification**. The most common method of identifying me is the use of a collar with a name tag and rabies license number. Tattoos or microchips are also available.

A collar with a tag is the least expensive. The tag should bear your name, address, phone number and my name. I should <u>always</u> wear my collar and tag. Should the collar damage my hair, change to a rolled leather collar.

A tattoo can be applied in about sixty seconds. The ink is indelible and can never be removed. Tattooing me requires that you register the tattoo to make it effective. To register a tattoo, to obtain information on the cost of a tattoo or to find an authorized tattooer, call one of the following:

Breeder's Action Board	I.D. Pet, Inc.	National Dog Registry
(313) 285-6311	(313) 243-9147	(800) NDR-DOGS

A microchip can be implanted between my shoulders by my veterinarian. The process is safe and relatively painless. However, a person or an agency finding me must have access to the correct scanner to detect the number code on the microchip. There are several brands of microchips each requiring its own scanner. For more information about microchips, call AVID, (800) 336-AVID or INFOPET, (800) INFOPET. Unfortunately, since microchips cannot be seen, they can be overlooked. In some cases a microchip may migrate. Consult my veterinarian about the pros and cons of microchips.

The following are tips to minimize the chances of my becoming lost or stolen:

- Use identification.
- Do not let me run free.
- Make sure gates and fences are secure.
- Have me neutered or spayed so I will not wander.
- Secure me during potentially frightening times, such as fireworks displays or thunderstorms.
- Keep me on a leash when walking with me.
- Secure car window and door locks when traveling with me.

If I should become lost or stolen, you may find it necessary to do one or more of the following:

- Drive and walk through our neighborhood calling my name and asking people if they have seen me.
- Place posters with my picture and description within a two mile radius of my home. Include your phone number and the fact that you are offering a reward. Give a poster to delivery people that frequent the neighborhood, and ask them to tell you if they see me, or better yet, to bring me home.
- Contact veterinary clinics, boarding kennels, humane societies and animal shelters, giving each a clear description and, if possible, a photo of me. Keep in touch every few days, since, if they do not have a picture, they may not recognize me from your description. If I am tattooed, tell the agencies. Give them a description of the tattoo. If I am microchipped, tell them where the chip is located and the brand.
- Place an ad in the newspaper and on the radio. Offer a reward.
- Contact laboratory facilities, local universities and hospitals to make sure that I have not been sold to them. Send a flyer with my photo to these facilities.
- Contact the highway department to inquire if an injured puppy has been found. If so, check to see if it is me.
- Call the police department if you think I have been stolen. You can also call the In Defense of Animals hot line, (800) 786-5367 for information about pet theft or for immediate assistance, call (415) 388-9641, extension 29.
- Check the yellow pages of your phone directory to determine if your city has a pet detective service that you might wish to use.
- Leave your name, phone number, picture and description of me with the motel/hotel mangement, or campground ranger and the local animal shelter, if I am lost while you are traveling and you must move on.

The American Humane Society and Sprint have a service that helps find lost dogs. The service tries to match the description of a found dog with the description given by the owner of a lost dog.

To report a lost dog call: (900) 535-1515. There is a charge for this call.

To report a found dog call: (800) 755-8111. There is no charge for this call.

When you find a lost dog without proper identification, check for a tattoo and take the dog to a veterinary facility or a humane society that has a scanner for microchips. If you place an ad in the newspaper, do not turn the dog over to anyone without proper verifiable information such as, veterinary records or a photo because there are unscrupulous people who claim dogs and sell them unlawfully.

SIX TO NINE MONTHS

I weigh _____ at six/seven months, _____ at seven/eight months

and _____ at eight/nine months.

I am _____ tall at six/seven months, _____ at seven/eight months,

and _____ at eight/nine months.

During these months I've learned: _____

_____

My favorite games are _____

_____

I started obedience school on _____

The name of my school is _____

My teacher's name is _____

I've learned the following at school: _____

_____

My teacher/owner taught me the following commands/tricks:

	Yes	No	I'm still working on it.
Come	____	____	____
Sit	____	____	____
Down	____	____	____
Stay	____	____	____
No	____	____	____
Off	____	____	____
Stand	____	____	____
Heel	____	____	____
Shake Paws	____	____	____
Sit up	____	____	____
Roll over	____	____	____
Bow	____	____	____

I have trained my owner to _____

MY GRADUATION CERTIFICATE, AWARD OR RIBBON FROM OBEDIENCE SCHOOL OR PHOTOS OF ME RESPONDING TO COMMANDS

A COMPARISON OF SENSES

My sense of taste is crude, but still I thrive;
No time to savor food and yet survive.
I wolf down all my food in haste,
So other dogs won't get a taste.
It's just an innate trick to stay alive!

I use my sense of touch like you use yours.
My touch alerts, inspects and reassures,
So when I touch you with my nose,
What does it mean, do you suppose?
A gesture that our friendship still endures?

My hearing versus yours is more acute;
A wider range of sound is at the root.
I turn my ears to zero in
At the exact sound origin.
My ears have a survival attribute.

Your world of pictures largely comes from sight;
Your eyes behold your world in colors bright.
Your life would lose some quality
If you were color blind like me.
And on this subject, let me shed some light.

My images come from my sense of smell,
And odors are the colors I know well.
I know by every critter's scent,
Just what it was, which way it went.
If it was friend or foe, my nose will tell!

PUPpourri

I sniffed out my first

squirrel at	_____ months.	raccoon at	_____ months.
rabbit at	_____ months.	toad at	_____ months.
cat at	_____ months.	turtle at	_____ months.
duck at	_____ months.	chipmunk at	_____ months.
opossum at	_____ months.	skunk at	_____ months.

Instead, I sniffed out a _____

When I chased a _____, this is what happened: _____

_____

_____

(Chasing animals is instinctive, but do not let me catch and kill them).

My owner was pleased, horrified, surprised. (circle one)

I sometimes stick my nose in/up _____

My owner was pleased, horrified, surprised. (circle one)

I tracked a _____

My owner is going to take me hunting when I am _____ months.

We are going to _____

I can carry _____ in my mouth.

I take it to _____

The things I like to do best are _____

_____

I saw my reflection in _____

I reacted by _____

AWS to consider

SPAYING AND NEUTERING. If I am female, spaying me is not only better for my health, but will make me easier to care for. You will not have to worry about the discharge, male dogs camping around our home for three weeks or personality changes when I am in heat.

If I am a male, neutering me will make me far less aggressive and dominant toward you and, therefore, easier to handle. As an unneutered male, my sex drive may interfere with training. It can make me prone to roam and cause me to mark my territory in our home by lifting my leg and urinating. I may also exhibit socially embarrassing behavior. I can impregnate a stray or unconfined female, creating unwanted puppies. If a stray female becomes pregnant, the puppies may be uncared for and die or become an additional burden for the community. Accidental mating should **never** be allowed to happen.

Spaying or neutering does not make me prone to obesity. Only overfeeding can accomplish that. I will be no less territorially protective. I will be no less effective in any job I have been trained to do. In fact, I will do a better job because I will be able to concentrate on activities you wish me to perform. If I am a female, I will be active year round since I will not be impeded by pregnancy or estrus. In general, spaying or neutering improves the overall longevity of most dogs, and it reduces breast and uterine cancers, prostate problems and testicular tumors.

According to the American Veterinary Medical Association, a female dog should be spayed before her first estrus or "heat" period (around six months of age.) A male dog can be neutered at six months to a year old. The timing for neutering and spaying may vary according to breed. Consult my veterinarian. Some veterinarians perform a canine vasectomy. This is recommended if there is a reason to preserve the dog's male appearance. Spaying and neutering surgeries are usually relatively inexpensive. However, if it is too costly for you, contact Spay/USA, (800) 248-SPAY for low-cost spay/neuter information.

I was spayed (date) _____

I was neutered (date) _____

I had a good recovery_____. I had the following problems

_____

_____

 AWS to consider

BREEDING. Real life, unfortunately, is not like the movie "101 Dalmatians." There are millions of puppies born every year and approximately ten million dogs are abandoned or destroyed each year. It is, therefore, extremely important to think it through before you decide to breed me. Breeding me can stress your energy and your pocketbook, and has no bearing on the quality of my life.

All of the following questions require a yes answer before considering breeding.

- Do I have such excellent qualities of breed that I must be bred to perpetuate them?
- Are there people who want my type of breed?
- Can you find good homes for all of my puppies, even those who do not perpetuate my fine qualities?
- If I am female, can you spend extra time, energy and financial resources to help me through any complications of pregnancy, such as a caesarean birth?

It is unrealistic to expect to make money from breeding me and selling my puppies. It will be a miracle if you come out even. Consider the following "built in" costs of breeding: veterinarian fees during my pregnancy; food for the puppies after weaning; inoculations; deworming; the cost of advertising the sale of the puppies; emergency veterinary care in case I have complications. There may also be unexpected demands on your time, like bottle feeding twenty-four hours a day if the puppies cannot be nursed.

Breeding a male dog will not make him a better house pet. In fact, he becomes more aggressive. He will be off at every opportunity in hot pursuit of the nearest female in heat. Overall, he will be harder to control. Breeding a female dog will not settle her down. (See PAWS to consider/SPAYING AND NEUTERING, page 94.)

If you feel your children must see the birth process to appreciate the miracle of life, buy a picture book or rent a video showing puppies being born. If you feel that I need a canine companion or you want more dogs, won't you please consider adopting or buying one of the countless homeless puppies or dogs in shelters across the country?

Carefully consider all of the previous factors. If you still decide to breed me and I am female, the following guidelines may be helpful. Buy and read a book on my breed that includes a section on breeding. Consult my veterinarian before allowing me to become pregnant. I should be in good health and free of all internal and external parasites. All of my inoculations should be up to date, so I can pass on immunity to disease to my puppies. If I am small, I may need to be x-rayed to make sure I will be able to have a normal delivery without a C-section. If I am overweight or too thin, I should not be bred. Determine the time of my first heat and do not allow me to mate at that time. Wait until my second or third heat when I will be more physically fit to bear puppies. However, mating should occur before I am three years old. Take a great deal of care in selecting the potential father of my litter. Let us become acquainted well in advance of breeding time. My veterinarian can determine the correct time for mating by taking a vaginal smear. This saves time and frustration. Check the calendar to see if you will be available to assist with whelping and caring for my pups and me during the first couple of weeks.

I may need vitamins or other nutritional needs during my pregnancy and while nursing. I will require double my usual amount of food during the latter stages of pregnancy and about three times as much when nursing. My food should be increased gradually. If I am eating a dry dog food, it is best to free-feed me during this time. In free-feeding, leave generous quantities of food in my bowl so I may eat at will. I will eat only what I need. My veterinarian may advise you to supplement the food with cooked liver or with a protein source, such as cottage cheese. Do not change foods or brands while I am pregnant since this can cause digestive problems. Do not bathe me near the end of my pregnancy. While I am pregnant, I should continue to be exercised in moderation so as not to cause injury. Walking is best.

My gestation period is generally fifty-eight to sixty-three days. Try to find responsible owners <u>before</u> my litter is born. After the puppies are born, they must be wormed, inoculated and receive check-ups. Do not sell my puppies until they are at least eight weeks old.

Well in advance of whelping seek advice from my veterinarian about the following:

1. How to assist with the whelping
2. What to do if there is a problem with the umbilical sac
3. How to clean the puppies if I am too tired
4. How to cut the umbilical cord
5. What to do with the placentas

The following is a partial list of equipment you will need for whelping. Consult my veterinarian for further needs.

1. A book on whelping.
2. Whelping box. Consult my veterinarian for the proper size box needed for my breed. Prepare the box two weeks in advance of delivery so I can get used to it. Place the box in a warm, secure area. A partition inside the box allows me to rest, separated from my puppies, yet near them. I will become anxious if the separation distance is too great.
3. Another box with a heating pad or hot water bottle and a blanket. Cover the heating pad or hot water bottle with the blanket. As the puppies are born, place them on the blanket. The heating pad should be kept on a low setting and my puppies should not be placed directly on the pad. Keep the box close so I will relax knowing you are trying to help.
4. A bottle of rubbing alcohol, iodine, scissors and a pan of warm soapy water, which will be needed for the whelping.
5. Washable towels for the box while puppies are nursing.
6. An ample supply of newspapers. These should be spread over the puppies' area for urine and excrement. The newspapers should be changed frequently.
7. A puppy nursing kit. Always use canine milk formula.
8. A record book to keep track of the birth weight and weekly weight of each puppy.
9. Nail clippers suitable for puppies. Nails should be cut so the puppies will not scratch me while they are nursing.
10. A list of local laws on buying and selling puppies.

The veterinarian will advise you about checking my temperature to determine the time of whelping. My temperature, taken rectally, is normal at 101 to 102 degrees Fahrenheit. A drop to 99 degrees Fahrenheit signals that whelping should occur within the next twenty-four hours. If it does not, consult the veterinarian immediately as there may be an obstruction. Prior to whelping, trim hair on my abdomen, back legs and nipple area which might interfere with the delivery and wash my abdominal area carefully with warm water. When the puppies start coming, stand by. Do not interfere unless necessary. Do not have many observers or I may become agitated.

The puppies should be born about every twenty minutes. If there is a period longer than one hour, take me outside for a little exercise. Give me time for elimination and a drink of water, then return me to the whelping box. If I am unsuccessful in continuing the birthing process, call my veterinarian. Within twenty-four hours of my delivery, take me to the veterinarian for an injection to rid the uterus of afterbirth.

When the whelping is finished, take me outdoors for elimination, some water and a short walk. After I have rested, I can resume my regular eating and drinking routine. Then, change the papers in the whelping box and reunite me with my puppies. You may notice a slight discharge for several weeks after I have given birth. Dog sanitary pads are commercially available. If you notice fresh blood, call my veterinarian.

Make sure that each puppy has a chance to nurse. My milk contains antibodies that help protect the puppies against disease during their first three months of life. Find a way to indentify each puppy in order to keep track of which ones have or have not nursed. Record each puppy's weight. If all the puppies are not getting enough to eat, you can supplement with a simulated canine milk product. However, be sure that every puppy has a turn with me during the first twenty-four hours. When supplementing the feeding, do not use an eyedropper. Use a nipple suitable for the size of the puppy.

The room temperature for the puppies should be kept at 85 to 90 degrees Fahrenheit during the first ten days of life, and then gradually lowered to normal room temperature. Leave my puppies and me alone as much as possible during the first three weeks. Handling the puppies too often may injure or infect them. Our area should contain low lighting until ten days after the puppies' eyes have opened. The eyes generally open between the tenth and fourteenth day. Dew claws can be removed by the veterinarian when the puppies are two to five days old. From three to five weeks, semi-solid food can be given but check first with my veterinarian. The puppies' food should be mixed with water or canine milk to the consistency of a thick milk shake. By eight weeks the puppies should be completely weaned.

Help my puppies' future owners by starting good housetraining habits. As soon as my puppies can walk, provide a separate papered area for elimination. At about three or four weeks of age, the puppies' feces must be checked by the veterinarian for worms. At that time consult my veterinarian about when to begin inoculations.

By now you should have found good, loving homes for most of my puppies. Conscientious breeders do not sell their puppies to just anyone who comes to them with a checkbook in hand. Ask for references even if you decide not to charge for my puppies. Be willing to take a puppy back if it is not a good match for its new family or if it develops a genetic defect.

Make sure that I skip one breeding period before becoming pregnant again. I need time to regain my strength, replace calcium and return my reproductive organs to normal. Occasionally, false pregnancies occur. The signs are nesting, swollen mammary glands and mothering a small object. If this occurs, consult my veterinarian.

PUPpourri

My owner chose to permit me to become a parent.

I became a mommy/daddy (date) _____

I had _____ puppies.

_____ males and _____ females.

My puppies went to the following loving people: _____

_____

_____

_____

_____

PHOTO OF MY LITTER

AWS to consider

SHOW TIME. Dog shows are designed to pick the best of the breed. The winners are used in selective breeding programs to improve the overall breed. The two primary dog clubs in the United States are the American Kennel Club and the United Kennel Club. For information on enrolling me in a show, write or call the American Kennel Club, 51 Madison Avenue, New York, NY 10010, 212-696-8200 or United Kennel Club, 100 East Kilgore Road, Kalamazoo, MI 49001-5597, 616-343-9020. I must be registered in order to compete.

Usually, the earliest a puppy can enter a show is six months of age. But even if you do not plan to show me, you may want to attend a dog show. As well as having fun, you will pick up pointers on dog care and my particular breed.

"A Beginner's Guide to Dog Shows" can be secured by writing to the American Kennel Club, 5580 Centerview Drive, Raleigh, NC 27606 or by calling, 919-233-9767.

My AKC or UKC registration number is _____

My first show (date) _____ at _____

I entered in the _____ class.

I performed the following: _____

_____

The judges said _____

I received a _____

I need to practice _____

My owner needs to practice _____

DOG TYPES?

Bird-dog, bandog, sled dog, carriage dog;
Coach dog, firedog, fogdog, prairie dog;

Gun dog, hangdog, hot dog, chilidog;
Lap dog, moon dog, sundog, silly dog;

Police dog, sea dog, top dog, underdog;
Wolf dog, watch dog, sheep dog, wonder dog!

PHOTOS OF MY FIRST SHOW <u>OR</u> JUST SHOWING OFF

NINE TO TWELVE MONTHS

I weigh _____ at nine/ten months, _____ at

ten/eleven months, and _____ at eleven/twelve months.

I am _____ tall at nine/ten months, _____ at

ten/eleven months, and _____ at eleven/twelve months.

During these months, I've learned: _____

_____

_____

I get the upper paw by _____

_____

When I want to go outside, I signal my owner by barking _____, whining _____,

sniffing the floor _____, appearing restless _____,

pawing at the door _____, vocalizing _____,

or standing by the door _____

The smartest things I do are _____

_____

I like to take _____

out of the wastepaper basket.

After I take it out, I _____

I like to drink water from _____

I like to play with crickets, grasshoppers, bees, butterflies or _____

My best animal friends are _____

_____

My best people friends are _____

_____

PHOTOS WITH MY BEST ANIMAL AND PEOPLE FRIENDS

STRUTTING MY STUFF WITH FRIENDS

I'm silky, white and cuddly, just a little ball of fluff;
I have a natural tendency to like to strut my stuff.

When walking with my people, I hear someone say, "How cute!"
In stature, I'm halfway between a mouse and malamute.

When I'm with dogs, I dominate, in doggie dialog.
It's not my size, but **confidence**, that lets me be top dog!

My big dog friend is overweight and not in good condition,
To tussle with **The DYNAMO** - that's me by definition!

I jump on him, run under him and simply just confound him;
I see him in the park, and then run circles all around him.

I'm one hot dog 'til someone says, "Now that is quite enough.
You'll rest until tomorrow, then you'll strut your puppy stuff!"

WAYS I STRUT MY PUPPY STUFF

_____

_____

_____

_____

_____

_____

_____

_____

_____

_____

_____

_____

_____

_____

_____

_____

_____

_____

_____

_____

_____

_____

PAWS to consider

BEHAVIORAL PROBLEMS. Some common behavioral problems we dogs have are barking excessively, biting, car chasing, destructive chewing (see PAWS to consider/ CHEW-ING, page 59), digging, dominance, elimination problems, fear of loud noises, hyperactivity, mounting and separation anxiety. Most of our behavioral problems are not severe and may be only bad habits. It is best to nip any problems in the bud. Sometimes all that is needed is the timely use of the word "no" or a few weeks of consistent and firm training. Addressing the problem one minute and looking the other way the next minute sends conflicting messages. I will lose confidence in you as my leader. Many dogs are abandoned or given away because their owners did not take the time to properly train or retrain them. If a problem has grown beyond your control, consult my veterinarian, a dog trainer/behaviorist or a book specifically about canine behavior problems. The following are a few problem solving suggestions.

BARKING. Barking is my normal response to various situations. I bark to protect my territory, in play, to let you know I need to go outside, to get your attention or that of another dog, or because I am bored or lonely (see LONELINESS, page 110). Some breeds have a tendency to bark more than others. It is only when my barking becomes excessive that it is a problem. When I am barking inappropriately, try one of the following two strategies.

1. Put a few coins or pebbles in an empty soft drink can and tape the opening. Each time I bark for no apparent reason, toss the can near me taking care not to hit me. Do not let me see you toss the can since you do not want me to associate anything frightening with you. The can is intended to startle and distract me from barking. Once you throw the can, say "Quiet!," followed by my name. Then console and make me think that **you** have just rescued me from something awful! Distract me to another activity.

2. Every time my barking is an annoyance, call me to you and say firmly, "Quiet!," followed by my name. Calm me and release me. Eventually, I will look to you each time to see if it is alright to bark. You must be persistent with this method.

If I have a tendency to bark needlessly, do not teach me to "speak." Do not scold or discipline me if I have been stimulated to bark during play or for some other reason. If I bark at passing people while we are walking in public, give a short tug on my leash, saying the word "Quiet." When I bark to tell you I have to go out, praise me. Similarly, praise me when I bark to let you know that someone is at the door. Once the caller is inside the home, use the "quiet" command to tell me it is ok. When I bark at something outside the home, say "Good puppy," and quiet me. Then investigate to determine the cause of my barking.

BITING. Biting can have serious consequences. It is important to immediately discourage biting behavior whether it occurs in young puppies or older dogs. I may want to bite for many reasons, such as protecting my possessions and food or because of pain from injury or grooming. If you suspect an injury, consult my veterinarian. During puppyhood, do not let me chew on your fingers. Do not put your fingers in my mouth in play or while I am teething. If I bite your hand, say, "Ouch!," in a very loud, high pitched voice, similar to the way a puppy would yelp. I assure you, this tactic will get my attention. Follow with a firm, "No bite!" Calm me and resume our friendship.

CAR CHASING. As a city dog, the only way I can chase a car is if I am allowed to roam free. When I am outside I should be confined to my yard, kennel or to a twenty foot tie-out in a shaded area. Puppies that roam free are a nuisance and can easily be injured. Those of us who roam, may eventually develop the habit of chasing cars, and one day will probably be hit. This will solve the problem of car chasing but not in a manner that would be to our liking. As a country dog, I may become a car chaser when allowed to run free. For my safety and your peace of mind, confine me to a fenced area or to a twenty foot tie-out in a shaded spot. If you insist in letting me run free, train me not to chase cars. Put me on a long lead and then have someone drive a car by our property. If I start to chase the car, shout, "No," and immediately give a quick, short, downward jerk to my lead. Call me to you and give me a treat. Repeat the procedure several times each day until you feel I understand the command. However, when I am running free, there is no guarantee that in the future I may not resort to car chasing. (The authors feel strongly that a city or country dog should <u>never</u> be allowed to run free in an unprotected area.)

DESTRUCTIVE CHEWING. The need to chew can be intense and is necessary for me during the first year or two of my life. During these periods, it is important to have safe chew toys for me. Replace chew toys as soon as they start to wear out. To keep me from chewing your things while you are away, confine me to my crate or a safe area. Leave chew toys and fresh water for me. When you return home, exercise me. Exercise helps to eliminate pent-up energy and boredom. When you see me chewing something that is unacceptable, immediately say, "No chew!," and take the item from me. Give me a chew toy and eventually I will learn what I can and cannot chew. As I grow older, my desire to chew will lessen. This varies by breed. Even if I am chewing less often, continue to provide safe chew toys on a regular basis. If my chewing is excessive after one year of age, check with my veterinarian. My diet may be inadequate.

DIGGING. Some of us dig in the yard or garden with such enthusiasm that it seems as if we are trying to strike oil. A persistent digger can transform a Garden of Eden into a lunar landscape. If you treasure the beauty of your lawn and garden, consider some of the following suggestions to curtail the mischief of the digger.

If you lack a dog enclosure, give me my own shaded space in the yard where I am permitted to dig. To insure that I remain in that area while outdoors, keep me on a tie-out lead. An effective tie-out lead is one that is attached to a stainless steel cork-screw stake. It should be at least twenty feet long. Twist the stake into the ground in a location where I will be shaded but will not become entangled in bushes, trees or other obstacles. I must have access to shelter and water while restrained.

If you do catch me digging in your favorite flower bed or garden area, shout a loud "No!" and divert me to another activity. Fill the hole halfway with soil. Put a flat rock, which is approximately the same size as the hole, into it and finish filling the hole with soil. When I try to re-open the hole, the rock will prevent me. Consider burying the nozzle end of the garden hose just below the surface of a hole that you have just filled. When you see me approach the spot to re-open the hole, turn on the water at the faucet or spigot. The blast of water will discourage all but the most persistent dogs.

(To keep Chip from digging in the flower beds, his owners installed invisible fencing. After a few weeks of training, Chip knew his boundary area so well that he could practically tell which blade of grass was the ultimate limit of his boundary.

Nevi's owners bought some inexpensive picket fencing and put it around their flower beds, an area where Nevi was very fond of digging. As a puppy, this kept Nevi out of these areas and he outgrew or forgot about his need to dig. As an adult dog in pursuit of a rabbit, Nevi clears this fencing easily when the rabbit squeezes between the pickets. Once in the garden he never stops to dig, since chasing the bunny is much more fun. He quickly jumps back over the picket fence and continues the merriment until the bunny is safely outside the property fence. Since bunny and Nevi seem to travel at close to the speed of light, the flowers miraculously survive.)

DOMINANCE. Dominant behavior is expressed by snapping, biting, growling, muttering or otherwise asserting dominance over you. If I exhibit this type of behavior, you will need to establish yourself kindly but firmly as my pack leader. One way to accomplish this is to behave like my mama. When I show signs of dominance, make direct eye contact with me, followed by a long, low growl. Immediately, after the growl, say "No!" You may feel foolish but, accept for the word "No," this is similar to what my mama would do when I misbehaved. My mama never shook her paw at me or hit me with a newspaper. You should follow her example, as these actions will frighten me, causing me to become defensively more dominant. You need to gain my respect, not fear. If I am a male with a tendency toward dominance, neutering me will reduce the tendency. If I continue to exhibit aggressive behaviors, seek advice from my veterinarian or a dog behavorist <u>immediately</u>. Never allow me to get away with dominant behavior toward you when I am a puppy, because as an adult dog my dominance can become dangerous.

I may sometimes growl or bite in play, but you will recognize the difference between playfulness and aggression. If I am prone to dominant tendencies, do not play aggressive games like tug-of-war with me.

ELIMINATION PROBLEMS. Excitement, fear, submissiveness, anxiety or disease may cause me to urinate or defecate involuntarily. When I urinate from excitement, such as a visitor's arrival, try to anticipate this occurrence and take proper precautions. Take me outside to urinate before a visitor arrives or keep me on a washable floor. When submissiveness is the cause, the problem will generally disappear with age. An action on your part may be too aggressive, causing me to become more submissive. Try to determine what you may be doing to aggravate the problem. Then stop doing it! When separation anxiety or fear is the cause, you must solve the problem to stop the behavior. Failing to find a cause may indicate that I have a physical problem that should be checked by my veterinarian.

FEAR OF LOUD NOISES. Many puppies are afraid of loud noises. We usually bark in response to our fear. Sometimes we are afraid because we cannot see what is making a noise. If it is the neighbor mowing the lawn, it may be sufficient to let me see what the neighbor is doing in order to quiet me. Never punish me for this fear. Punishment will just make me more fearful. Sometimes I am afraid because a loud noise, such as a firecracker, may hurt my ears. If that is the case, take me to a safe place away from the noise. Leave my favorite toy with me. When the noise has ended, come back for me and give me lots of love. Some authorities on behavior believe you can desensitize me to loud noises. There are several sound effect tapes sold in music stores. These tapes contain thunderstorms or other loud noises. Take me to the room with your stereo speakers, bringing along some special treats and my favorite toy. Play the tape at a volume that is hardly audible to you. I have much keener hearing than you do. As the tape plays give me a treat and reassure me. Play with me for about fifteen minutes. Do this everyday while increasing the volume until it is very loud. When I seem less fearful, play the tape loudly but do your own thing and don't play with me. During the fifteen minutes call me and give me a treat to reassure me that everything is all right. Repeat this activity for several days until I seem comfortable with loud noises. Then discontinue the effort. If I become frightened again, repeat the process.

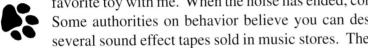

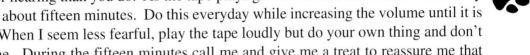

Should I be unable to adjust to loud noises, behavior modification medicines are available, or you can just accept the fact, and find a secure dark place where I can hide when noises frighten me. When the noise ends, comfort me and let me know that everything is all right. (Nevi's owners were able to help him adjust to loud noises but not to the vacuum sweeper. He solves the problem by removing himself to another room whenever it comes near him. Chip feels exactly the same as Nevi in regard to vacuum sweepers.)

HYPERACTIVITY. We puppies have a tremendous amount of energy, and some breeds, especially the working or hunting breeds, have even more. All of us require at least twenty minutes of exercise a day. If I am confined to my crate for two or more hours, the desire for exercise will be even stronger. Exercise or play is required several times a day. A walk, with time to investigate, is a good source of releasing energy. If the area is safe, a retractable leash that allows me to roam twelve to sixteen feet is an excellent way to increase my activity. After exercise, have a cool down period. Put me in the down position and stroke my belly saying, "Easy." Keep me quiet for five minutes. Each day gradually increase my cool down time until you reach thirty minutes. If I am exercised regularly but still seem to be hyperactive, consult my veterinarian. If I jump on people when they come to visit, teach me the off command. (See PAWS to consider/TRAINING, page 77.)

110

LONELINESS. Puppies by nature are pack animals. In the wild they communicate with their pack by their facial expressions, ears, scent glands, urine and tails. Since dogs have been domesticated, humans are their pack and provide much needed companionship.

I will become lonely if left alone all day. My loneliness can lead to destructive behavior, depression or excessive barking. A solution may be to buy a companion animal for me. However, wait until I am six months old before getting a second animal. I need time to bond with you. Should you decide to buy another dog, select one close to my size. It does not have to be the same breed, but our ages should be within two years of each other. Let us first meet on neutral ground, such as a park. Do not bring the second dog directly to our home because I may think it is invading my property. Neutered dogs or a female and male dog get along well. Having two dogs for companionship is usually fine. Having three dogs may cause two of them to pick on the third. If I am a dominant dog, it is best to find a submissive dog to be my companion since two dominant dogs may fight. Let me bond with the new dog before you interact with it. During my adjustment period, greet me first so I will not be jealous of the new dog. If after a few weeks we are not getting along, consider returning the second dog. Monitor us the first week to prevent fights.

Should you choose not to buy a companion dog, interact with me as soon as you come home. If you work, you may wish to hire a dog sitter to come once a day and exercise me and give me companionship or take me to a dog day care facility.

MOUNTING. Male and occasionally female puppies have a tendency to try to mount a person's leg. This is embarrassing for my owner. To discourage this behavior, shout "No!" and make direct eye contact. Remove and distract me with a toy. Mounting will be a problem as long as I am sexually active. Neutering me is the best solution.

SEPARATION ANXIETY. Puppies are very social animals. We sometimes suffer separation anxiety because we have not been properly trained or have been spoiled. Dogs that have been abandoned and are now rescued may show signs of separation anxiety until they acquire trust in their new owner. Separation anxiety can lead to other problems when I am alone, such as barking, howling, destructive chewing or urinating. Consider the following solution for this problem. Pretend you are leaving. Put on your coat, get your keys, say good bye, but do not leave. Do this several times a day. The next day, go through the same procedure but leave for five minutes. If I use a crate, place me in the crate before leaving. This will make me feel secure. Turn on the radio or television to keep me company. Turn on a light if it is dark. Talk to me for a few minutes before you leave to put me at ease. Then leave cheerfully saying, "Goodbye, I'll be back soon" or something similar. Say the same thing each time you leave. I will not understand the words, but I will associate those sounds with your leaving, and I will eventually know that you will return. Leave a safe chew toy for me. When you return, greet me and tell me that I was a good dog. Over the next two weeks, each time you leave, increase the time by a few minutes until you are away for an hour. This practice is similiar to how a mother dog behaves when weaning her puppies. It may take several weeks until I am comfortable being left alone.

DOG TALK

The happy dog that feels secure will walk with tail held high;
Or wag its tail in friendliness when greeting passersby.

Beware the angry, hostile dog that keeps its ears laid back.
Its lowered tail and bristled hair warn that it could attack!

The timid dog feels insecure and it may try to hide,
Or make a puddle on the floor or cower by your side.

Submissive dog rolls on its back. Its tummy is exposed.
It thinks of you as alpha dog and lies in this repose.

All dogs, whatever size and breed, from time to time may be,
Depending on the circumstance, each of these types you see.

PHOTOS OF ME WITH AN ATTITUDE!

PUPpourri

In unfamiliar situations I lean against my owner for security _____,

like to investigate _____, am fearful _____,

or I _____

I am afraid of:

_____ thunder   _____ sirens

_____ fireworks   _____ lawn mowers

_____ loud noises   _____ vacuum cleaners

_____ motorcycles   _____ broom/mop

When I am afraid, I hide under the _____, inside the _____,

beside the _____. I run and get my _____

I am comforted by _____

I am not afraid of any of the above, but I don't like _____

_____

When visitors come to my house, I _____

_____

I become very excited when _____

When I become very excited, I _____

When I am left alone, I _____

I like to watch _____ from the window.

I tried to protect my turf at _____ months because _____

_____

I was successful. (yes/no). I had second thoughts and hid behind my owner (yes/no).

My owner said, _____

I threw a temper tantrum when _____

because _____

ONE YEAR

I weigh _____.

I am _____ tall.

Now that I am all grown up, my owner describes my temperament as

calm _____, hyperactive _____, easily excited _____,

aggressive _____, aloof _____, friendly _____, lazy _____,

or _____

I celebrated my birthday with _____

I had a special treat of _____

For my birthday, I received _____

_____

_____

On my owner's birthday I gave him/her a _____

MY BIRTHDAY PHOTO

ADDITIONAL PHOTOS OF ME ALL GROWN UP

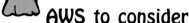
PAWS to consider

ONE YEAR AND BEYOND. I am now a young adult dog. Your training, consistency, patience, love and good care have helped me become a well-behaved, lovable friend who will be loyal to you for the rest of my life. At one year of age or older, I can be weaned to a nutritionally complete adult dog food that can be used for the next six or seven years. Check with my veterinarian for the appropriate timing for the change since this varies from one breed to another. Change my food gradually, mixing the new food with the old. Observe my stool for any problems. If I have problems converting, consult my veterinarian. If you are using dry food, you can now consider free-feeding me, which means filling my bowl daily with the correct amount of food for my size and leaving the food down all the time. At first, I may overeat but when I realize that the food is available all the time, I will soon regulate myself. Most of the time, dogs do not overeat dry dog food. If I do continue to overeat, return to measured portions twice a day. When using canned food, I can be fed twice a day in portions correct for my size. Add a few appropriate dog treats between meals. I must have fresh cool water available at all times indoors and outdoors.

Some male dogs between the ages of one and two become more assertive and, like a teenager, try to test your relationship. Be firm but kind in my training, and I will eventually outgrow this behavior. Establish the fact that you are still the leader of my pack.

At about seven years of age, I will start to grow old, which means my metabolism may change and I may need fewer calories. When my energy level begins to slow, use a nutritionally complete senior food for the remainder of my life. Consult my veterinarian about the change. Older dogs are more prone to disease, especially kidney disease, which is found to some degree in almost every dog over the age of eight. A diet that is lower in protein can help the problem. Older dogs urinate more frequently. If I have abnormal thirst, frequent or painful urination, blood in the urine, vomiting, diarrhea, constipation or painful bowel movements, take me to my veterinarian immediately. Even without any symptoms of old age, you may want to consult my veterinarian for advice on other problems of the older dog, such as the loss of hearing or eyesight. If I do lose my hearing or sight, you may find that this is not as debilitating to me as it is to humans. Dogs are olfactory animals and, therefore, depend most strongly on their sense of smell.

Sometimes, as an older dog, I may have accidents because I have problems maintaining good bladder and bowel control. Do not scold or punish me, for I will feel as badly about this as you do. A loss of bladder control may signal urinary track infection. Medication is available for incontinence, which is mainly a problem of older spayed female dogs. A loss of bowel control may indicate other illness. Provide papers in the house for me in case I cannot make it outdoors in time. Some older dogs will not use papers inside no matter how strongly the urge to eliminate. An ill or arthritic dog may have to be carried outside in order to eliminate.

Sometimes I may be cranky if awakened from a nap or startled. The crankiness may be from the pain of arthritis. Put yourself in my paws, and try to be patient. If I develop arthritis, make sure that my bed is in a warm area and not in a draft. If my bed is on the second floor of my home, provide a resting place on the first floor during the day so that I will not have to climb stairs. It may be necessary to carry me to my bed at night.

As an older dog, I may become set in my ways and a little stubborn. Try not to change my routine. Continue to exercise me daily, but remember, that as an older dog, I may tire more easily, may have arthritis and may not react as quickly. Therefore, be aware of potentially dangerous situations, especially when walking me. I may be less able to endure extremely hot or cold weather.

Give dog treats for rewards or for "dessert" and hard biscuits or beef hide chews to aid my dental care. It is important that grooming and dental care continue. Halitosis in an older dog can indicate diabetes or kidney disorders. When grooming, check the skin for warts or tumors. Older dogs are prone to develop them. If a tumor is found, take me to my veterinarian to make sure it is benign. Continue to monitor the tumor for change. If change occurs, check with my veterinarian. My toenails may need to be trimmed more often due to a decrease in exercise. After bathing me, be sure to keep me away from drafts for three to four hours, or until I am completely dry. I should be taken to the veterinarian yearly for a checkup. However, since I may develop problems as I grow older, it may be necessary to see the veterinarian more often.

If you are going to travel and have not placed me in a kennel before, consider hiring a dog sitter. As an older dog in a kennel, I will be greatly stressed by the separation from you and my home. I would be more comfortable at home in familiar surroundings.

DOGGY YEARS
(This is an average according to Connecticut veterinarian, Dr. George Whitney, who has studied canine aging.)

DOG		PEOPLE	DOG		PEOPLE
1 year	=	16 years	9 years	=	52 years
2 years	=	24 years	10 years	=	56 years
3 years	=	28 years	11 years	=	60 years
4 years	=	32 years	12 years	=	64 years
5 years	=	36 years	13 years	=	68 years
6 years	=	40 years	14 years	=	72 years
7 years	=	44 years	15 years	=	76 years
8 years	=	48 years	16 years	=	80 years

I'VE BEEN AROUND

Listen up, you puppies,
  I've some advice for you.
You, too, can breeze through puppyhood;
  I'll tell you what to do.

I've been around a long, long time;
  I'm worldly-wise, for sure.
You little guys are puppy fluff,
  So innocent, so pure!

I've learned some hard-luck lessons,
  And I've knowledge you can gain.
So trust me when I say that kissing kitties causes pain!

It's best to give them lots of room; don't ever try to nuzzle --
If you'll do this, they'll never sink their claws into your muzzle!

And when you're faced with big dogs who will stare you in the eye,
It's best to be submissive; just roll over, whine and cry!

Behave this way with bullies; try to stay out of their way.
You will grow big and strong and can defend your turf some day.

I've learned some hard-luck lessons, and you can look up to me,
For I have grown into the big and robust dog you see.

In living with your people, better let them have their way,
And learn your lessons well when they say "come," or "sit," or "stay."

It's bad enough to dig and uproot all the garden plants,
But never chew your owners' shoes or leave paw prints on their pants.

I've been around a long, long time and know just what to do,
For I am now a one-year-old and I'll take care of you!

YOUR FAVORITE STORY ABOUT ME

_____

_____

_____

_____

_____

_____

_____

_____

_____

_____

_____

_____

_____

_____

_____

_____

_____

_____

_____

_____

(We at Pallachip Pulbishing would love to read your story for possible future publication. See the order form in the back of the book for our address.)

PUPpourri

SPECIAL OCCASIONS.

On my first Christmas I was _____ old.

I received _____

I ate _____

I liked _____

I was attracted to the Christmas tree because _____

_____

I _____ the Christmas tree.

MY CHRISTMAS PICTURES

PHOTOS OF ME ENJOYING OTHER SPECIAL OCCASIONS

A DAY IN MY LIFE

My life is simply just a lark;
I seek adventure dawn 'til dark,
And never fail to leave my mark,
On field or woodland shrub and bark.

My people work with me each day,
And teach commands like "come" and "stay."
They give me lots of praise and say,
I am so good when I obey.

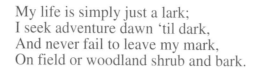

The tot is someone I adore,
For he drops crumbs upon the floor.
I track him down for treats galore,
My friend, the little cookie store.

The little girl and I have tea.
Her doll joins in and that makes three.
And when we chat, we all agree,
Tea parties are great fun, you see.

The boy's my pal; some things he likes
Are playing catch and riding bikes.
Just he and I, no lagging tykes,
When we explore or go on hikes.

I'll see my clinic vets at three,
And bring a color print of me,
To put in their menagerie,
Of snapshots of the pets they see.

I love to see that feisty cat
That bares its claws to make me scat;
I stand my ground and that is that,
Then whirl around and smooch that cat.

I wallow in an earthy scent,
Or follow where some critter went;
It's what I love; it's time well spent,
This doggy life for which I'm meant.

Tonight, my people looked askance;
My odor put them in a trance.
A bath would surely help enhance;
They'll have to catch me first....
FAT CHANCE!

A TYPICAL DAY IN MY LIFE

MY PUPFOLIO

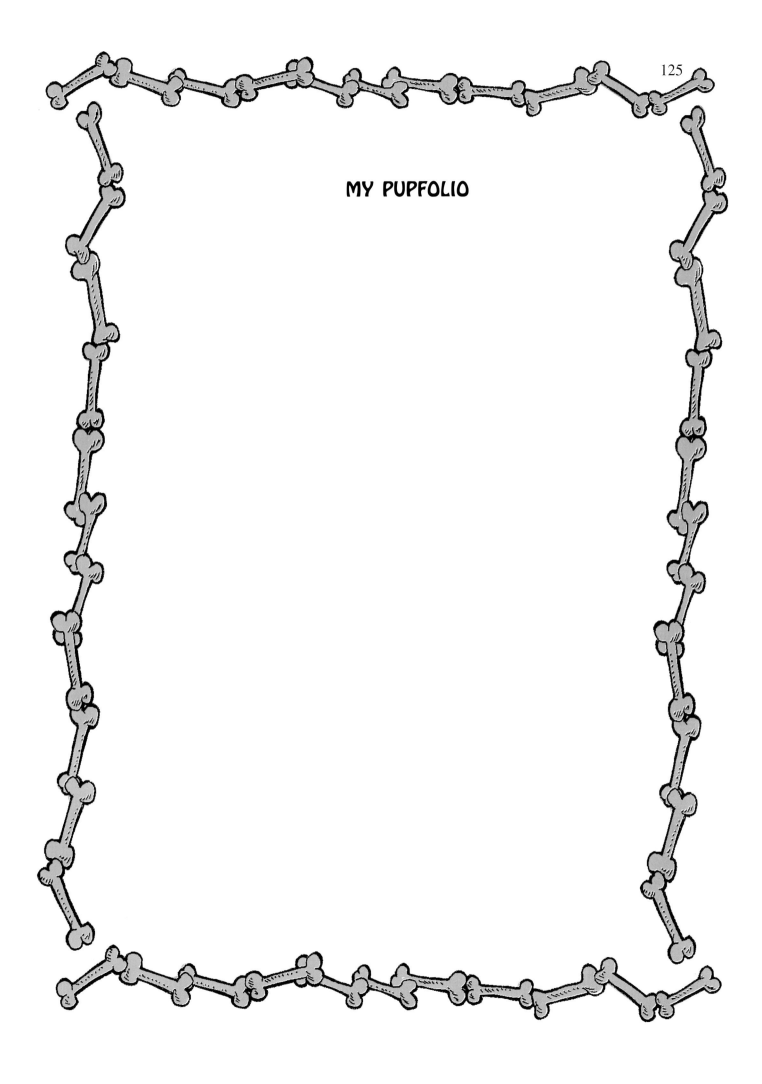

MY PUPFOLIO

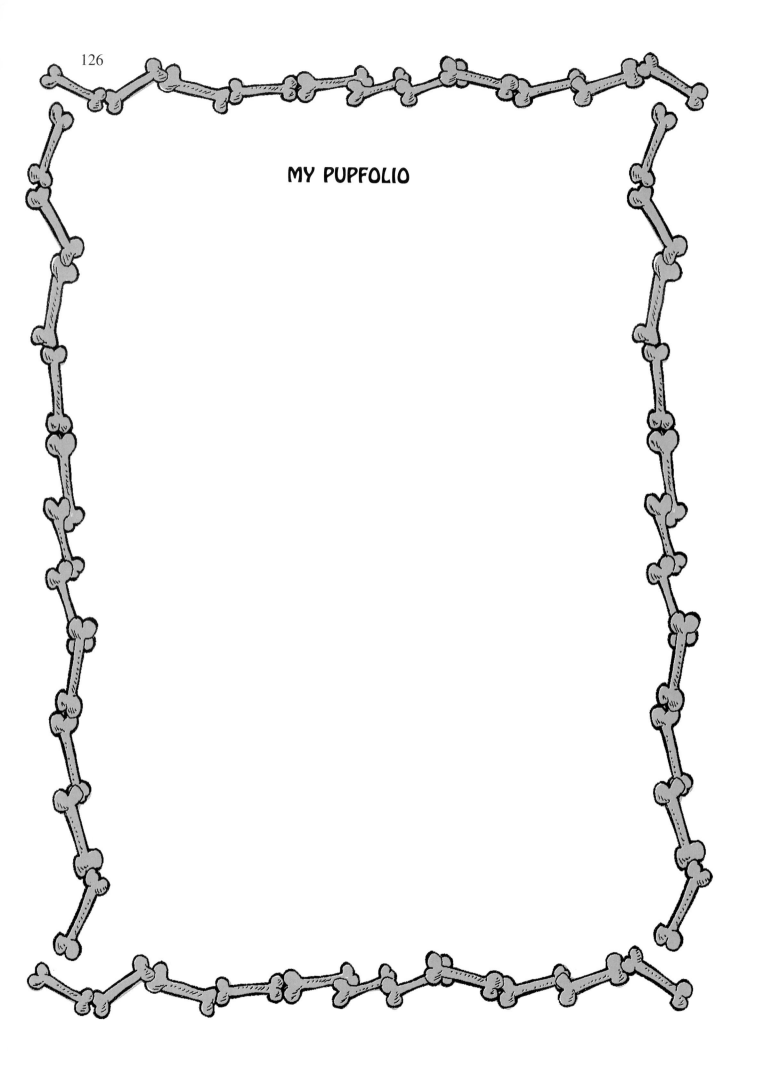

MY PUPFOLIO

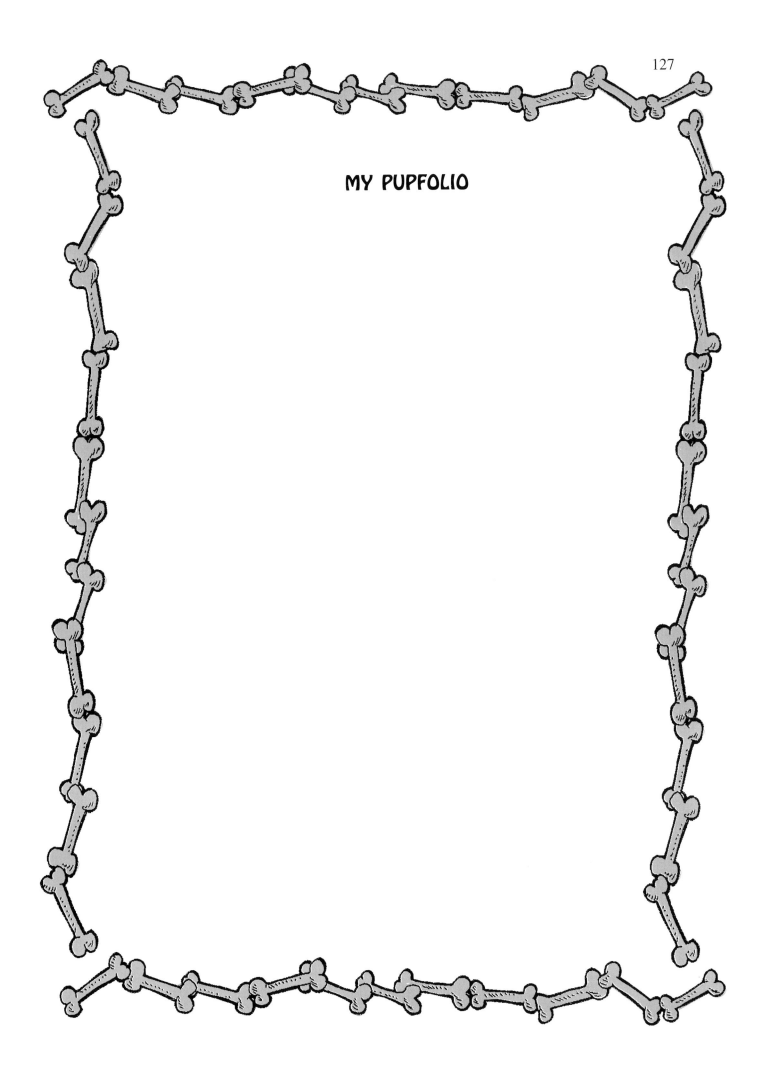

MY PUPFOLIO

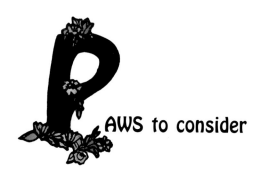

PAWS to consider

DYING. Since my expected life span is usually ten to eighteen years, it's unlikely that I will outlive you. You may, therefore, have to face the unpleasant thought of having me euthanized. This is very difficult for both you and me, but it is an event that must be faced. If I am ill, suffering, or have poor quality of life, do not wait too long to have me euthanized.

There is, however, the possibility that you may die before me. Making arrangements in your will can insure that I will be properly cared for in the event that this happens. By law you are not allowed to leave money to me since I am considered property. The money for my care should be left to a banking institution with instructions for my care.

I would like to offer the following suggestions when the time comes to have me "put to sleep." Upon taking me to the veterinarian, it is best for you to stay with me during the process. It will be very comforting to me, even though it will be hard for you. Hold me in your arms while the veterinarian sedates me. After I am asleep, the veterinarian will use a pentobarbital solution. This method keeps me from suffering and makes the whole process easier for me. If you do not think you can handle this, say your goodbyes, and then leave me with my trusted veterinarian. Children need to be told what is going to happen to me. Be sure that they understand the meaning of the words "put down," "put to sleep," or euthanized, and also, that they were not the cause of my leaving. If you have other pets, offer them comfort since they will miss me as much as you and may grieve my loss.

After I have been euthanized, you can take care of my body in one of the following ways.

1. My veterinarian can dispose of my body. This may be done in a communal cremation. If you wish a private cremation, this can be arranged and an urn or box for my remains can be ordered through my veterinarian or a pet cemeterian.
2. You can take me home and bury me. However, before doing this, it is best to check your city regulations. When burying me you can use a box or purchase an air-tight pet casket through my veterinarian or pet cemeterian. Usually the caskets can be dug up and moved if you relocate and wish to have me buried at the new location. When burying me, you should have two feet of compacted soil above my box or casket. This will keep other animals from digging up the box.
3. You can take me to a pet cemetery. For information on pet cemeteries or crematories contact:

International Association of Pet Cemeteries
1-800-952-5541

You may feel grief when I die no matter what the cause of death might have been. Whether I have been your pet for a short time or for many years, I have been a valued member of the family. I will be sadly missed. At this time it is important to have friends and family near who understand and are sensitive to the grief you may be feeling. Do not expect everyone to know how saddened you are by my loss. Well meaning friends who have never owned a dog might try to cheer you up by remarking that, "It was only a dog!" Don't be too offended because they just do not understand. Grieving is natural, but if you have problems coping, ask my veterinarian for phone numbers of a pet grief hotline. There are several throughout the country. A few of these numbers are included below.

The American Veterinary Medical Association (AVMA) has published two brochures called "Pet Loss How Do I Know When It Is Time" and "When Your Animal Dies Understanding Your Feeling of Loss." They are free and can be obtained by writing AVMA, 1931 N. Meacham Road, Suite 100, Schaumburg, Illinois 60173. The Chicago Veterinary Medical Association (CVMA) has published a brochure called "Losing a Special Companion: Resolving the Grief, Remembering the Good." The brochure is free and can be secured by writing to the CVMA, 161 South Lincolnway, North Aurora, Illinois 60542. The CVMA also has a Pet Loss Support Hotline. The number is on the brochure. Veterinarians at the University of California operate a Pet Loss Support Hotline. They can be reached daily from 6:30 p.m. to 9:30 p.m. Pacific Standard Time at 916-752-4200.

(There is not much that we, the authors, can offer to you to make your dog's death easier except the knowledge that the passage of time eases the pain. We know, because we have walked this path before. In fact, even with the passage of time, it was difficult for us to write this section. It is a heartbreaking time, but hopefully, the stories and the photos that you have preserved in this book will bring fond memories.)

I hope you will eventually feel like owning another dog. Although it will not take my place, it will have its own unique personality and bring you as much happiness as I have.

MY HEALTH CARE RECORD

INOCULATIONS/TESTS
(Place a check mark to indicate inoculations and tests have been given.)

DATE GIVEN	__	__	__	__	__	__	__	__	__
DISTEMPER	__	__	__	__	__	__	__	__	__
HEPATITIS	__	__	__	__	__	__	__	__	__
PARAINFLUENZA	__	__	__	__	__	__	__	__	__
LEPTOSPIROSIS	__	__	__	__	__	__	__	__	__
PARVOVIRUS	__	__	__	__	__	__	__	__	__
CORONAVIRUS	__	__	__	__	__	__	__	__	__
BORDETELLA	__	__	__	__	__	__	__	__	__
LYME	__	__	__	__	__	__	__	__	__
RABIES	__	__	__	__	__	__	__	__	__
WORMING	__	__	__	__	__	__	__	__	__
HEARTWORM	__	__	__	__	__	__	__	__	__

MY HEALTH CARE RECORD

INOCULATIONS/TESTS
(Place a check mark to indicate inoculations and tests have been given.)

DATE GIVEN   ___ ___ ___ ___ ___ ___ ___ ___ ___

DISTEMPER   ___ ___ ___ ___ ___ ___ ___ ___ ___

HEPATITIS   ___ ___ ___ ___ ___ ___ ___ ___ ___

PARAINFLUENZA   ___ ___ ___ ___ ___ ___ ___ ___ ___

LEPTOSPIROSIS   ___ ___ ___ ___ ___ ___ ___ ___ ___

PARVOVIRUS   ___ ___ ___ ___ ___ ___ ___ ___ ___

CORONAVIRUS   ___ ___ ___ ___ ___ ___ ___ ___ ___

BORDETELLA   ___ ___ ___ ___ ___ ___ ___ ___ ___

LYME   ___ ___ ___ ___ ___ ___ ___ ___ ___

RABIES   ___ ___ ___ ___ ___ ___ ___ ___ ___

WORMING   ___ ___ ___ ___ ___ ___ ___ ___ ___

HEARTWORM   ___ ___ ___ ___ ___ ___ ___ ___ ___

MY HEALTH CARE RECORD

ILLNESSES OR INJURIES

Date: _____

Treatment: _____

Home Care Instructions: _____

_____

_____

Date: _____

Treatment: _____

Home Care Instructions: _____

_____

_____

Date: _____

Treatment: _____

Home Care Instructions: _____

_____

_____

Date: _____

Treatment: _____

Home Care Instructions: _____

_____

_____

Date: _____

Treatment: _____

Home Care Instructions: _____

_____

_____

MY HEALTH CARE RECORD

RESULTS OF WORMING:

Date & Instructions: _____

_____

Date & Instructions: _____

_____

Date & Instructions: _____

_____

Date & Instructions: _____

_____

OTHER MEDICATIONS:

Date & Instructions: _____

_____

Date & Instructions: _____

_____

Date & Instructions: _____

_____

Date & Instructions: _____

_____

Date & Instructions: _____

_____

SPECIAL NOTES ABOUT ME

_____

_____

_____

_____

_____

_____

_____

_____

_____

_____

_____

_____

_____

_____

_____

_____

_____

_____

_____

_____

_____

_____

_____

_____

_____

SOME DOGGONE GOOD ADVICE

ADMINISTERING MEDICINES

Medication should be given only on the advice of my veterinarian. The easist way to give me a pill is to put the pill inside a bite-sized ball of flavorful food. Check with my veterinarian to determine which foods are compatible with the medication I am taking. Another method is to put me in a sitting position. If I am small, placing me on a table in the sit position gives better access. Stand behind me and place the thumb and fingers of one hand on either side of my snout behind my canine teeth. The canines are the two longest teeth on either side of my mouth. Talk to me in soothing tones while gently pulling the top of my snout upward in order to open my mouth. Do not attempt to open my mouth by pulling down on my lower jaw. You will be unable to open my mouth properly and may hurt me. Once my mouth is open, hold the pill between the thumb and forefinger of your other hand, and gently lower my bottom jaw with your remaining three fingers of that hand. Place the pill as far back on my tongue as possible. Close my mouth and hold it gently while tipping my snout slightly upward. With your other hand, rub the front of my neck to stimulate swallowing. Practice this procedure a few times by placing a piece of tasty food in my mouth. This will help me to more readily accept the pill later.

To give medicine in liquid form, place me in the sit position. If I am small, put me on a table in the sit position for better access. Talk soothingly to me. Using a nonbreakable liquid medicine dispenser, fill the dispenser with the proper amount of medication. Pull outward on the loose skin on the <u>side</u> of my bottom jaw. This will act as a funnel. Release the medication. Quickly but gently place your hand around my muzzle in order to keep my mouth closed. Tilt my head slightly upward while stroking my neck with your other hand until I swallow the medication. If I start to choke or cough, lower my head immediately. Do not disperse liquid medicine into the front of my mouth as this can sometimes cause aspiration pneumonia.

ALLERGIES

Signs of allergies in dogs are sneezing, watery eyes, chewing or licking the paws, skin reactions, chronic itching, vomiting and/or diarrhea. The most common types of allergies are flea and atopy (inhalant allergy). Less common are food or contact allergies.

A flea allergy can cause hair loss and skin lesions that must be treated. The ongoing process of controlling fleas in my area is very important. Flea allergies generally become more severe as I grow older. (See PAWS to consider/EXTERNAL PARASITES, page 54.) It is important to contact my veterinarian if you suspect a flea allergy.

Atopy allergies are generally seasonal. This type of allergy may cause me to rub my face on the floor or furniture, scratch myself or lick my feet. Allergy testing can identify the allergens I am allergic to. The allergens, once identified, should be avoided.

136

Contact allergy can be caused by plants or home furnishings. Signs of this type of allergy are itchy skin and hair loss. As in the case of flea or atopy allergy, the best solution is to avoid the allergens.

Food allergies may cause itching, gastrointestinal upset or skin lesions. Food allergies can be caused by many different foods.

If allergies are suspected, it is important that I be tested by my veterinarian so the offending allergens can be identified and eliminated.

Sometimes owners become allergic to their dogs. It is the dander, tiny particles of loose skin or hair, that causes the allergy. Controlling the dander helps to control the allergy. Dander can be reduced by vacuuming the home frequently, washing the area where I live, brushing or combing me daily and shampooing me with a quality pet shampoo. Shampooing must be done often, but not so often that it depletes my natural oils. There is a body rinse available from my veterinarian that, applied to my coat, neutralizes the allergy producing dander.

FIRST AID KITS

The following is a list of suggestions for a doggy first aid kit. When vacationing with me, take the kit with you in the car. The products included in your kit can be purchased at hardware, pharmacy or specialty shops. Generic brands are usually less costly than name brands.

A FIRST AID BOOK FOR DOGS. Consult the first aid book before using first aid products or tools.

TOOLS
small needle-nosed pliers
pointed tweezers
small wire cutters
magnifying glass
blunt-nosed scissors
non-breakable rectal thermometer
penlight flashlight
eye dropper

ANTIBACTERIAL AGENTS
povidone iodine solution (for disinfecting wounds)
neomycin-polymyxin-bacitracin topical ointment
hospital antiseptic solution
3% hydrogen peroxide solution for cleaning dirt and blood from a wound
Boric acid solution
(do not use antibiotic ointment in the ears or eyes)

DRESSINGS
non-stick wound pads 2x2", 3x3", 4x4"
gauze squares
rolled gauze 1x2" wide for making a muzzle in case of serious injury, or wrapping bandaged wounds
cotton-tip swabs
cotton balls
adhesive tape
(Grannicks' Bitter Apple® can be sprayed on bandages and around wounds to deter me from interfering with the healing process.)

FOOD FOR ILL PUPPIES

There is a highly nutritional, palatable pudding like food made by Hill's Pet Nutrition, Inc. called Hill's® Prescription Diet® Canine/Feline a/d®. If I am recovering from surgery and am unable to eat on my own, this food can be fed to me with a syringe. The food is very appetizing. Consult my veterinarian for more information about this food or similar foods produced by other manufacturers.

HEAT STRESS AND HEATSTROKE

The signs of heat stress include increased heart rate, panting and red mucous membranes. My nose, ears and legs will feel hot. If this occurs, I should be taken into an air conditioned area immediately to cool down. I will need cool water to drink. If I can not be taken inside, hose me down with cool water. Heat stress can lead to heatstroke.

The signs of heatstroke are panting, rapid pulse, fever and drooling. I may also vomit, have diarrhea or collapse. If left unattended, I can become dehydrated and can go into shock or coma. If you suspect that I am suffering from heatstroke, immerse me, up to my neck in cold water to lower my temperature. Then wrap me in a wet towel and take me to my veterinarian.

Never leave me in a car during the summer months. Cars heat up quickly and I can suffer from heatstroke. Provide shaded protected areas outdoors and plenty of water for me. Cement floored pens can heat up quickly.

Do not exercise me on an extremely hot day. In summer, exercise me in the early morning or late evening when it is cool.

MOIST DERMATITIS

Moist dermatitis or "hot spots" occur during the summer months. Dogs with dense coats are more prone to this condition. The skin will be inflamed, extremely itchy and hot. The area may become bald. These "spots" can be the result of anything that irritates the skin, such as an allergic reaction to food, sensitivity to flea bites, matted hair or a skin infection. Consult my veterinarian before treating this condition.

POISONS

Keep plants and garden products away from me. A list of poisonous and non-poisonous plants can be secured from the National Animal Poison Control Center, University of Illinois College of Veterinary Medicine, 2001 S. Lincoln Ave. Urbana, Illinois 61801. The cost is $10.00 and checks should be made payable to NAPCC. If I have ingested a poisonous substance, call my veterinarian immediately.

Do not leave medications or foods intended for humans where I can reach them. Some are very toxic. Aspirin substitutes can kill me. Do not leave my medicines or foods in areas where I can reach them since unmeasured quantities of these could be toxic.

Never give me alcohol. Take extreme precautions to keep me away from antifreeze products. Both are toxic even in small amounts.

Keep me off lawns that have been newly fertilized. (Check product precautions regarding my safety.)

SKUNKS

Should I be unfortunate enough to have an encounter with a skunk, remove my collar, harness and any clothing I may be wearing and throw them away. Use clean warm water to flush my eyes. A few drops of warm olive oil in my eyes relieves the stinging sensation caused by the skunk's spray. Bathe me using dog shampoo and then rinse me in tomato juice or diluted lemon juice. Repeat the process. It will take several days before the odor is completely gone. Odor neutralizers are sold in some pet stores. Skunks can be carriers of rabies. If for some reason, I have not been vaccinated for rabies, take me to my veterinarian for evaluation.

SWIMMING

Bathe me after I have been swimming in salt water or chlorinated water. Never leave me unattended when I am swimming as I can tire easily. Do not force me to swim for some breeds are averse to swimming. When oceanside, beware of jellyfish and sea lice. Drinking seawater will make me ill.

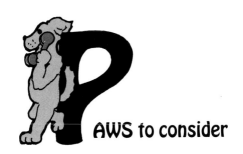

AWS to consider

139

NOTABLE NUMBERS AND ADDDRESS

Animal Shelter: _____

Canine Insurance Company:_____

Humane Society: _____

My Groomer: _____

My Kennel:

    Name: _____

    Address: _____

    _____

    Phone: _____

    Kennel Owner's Name: _____

My Sitter: _____

My Veterinarian: _____

Newspaper Classified (Lost Pet Service): _____

Pet Shop: _____

Poison Control Center: _____

Police Department: _____

24 Hour Emergency Pet Clinic: _____

For information on registering me, if I am a purebred dog, write or call the following:

American Kennel Club
5580 Centerview Drive
Raleigh, NC 67606
919-233-9767

United Kennel Club
100 East Kilgore Road
Kalamazoo, MI 49001-5597
616-343-9020

142

ABOUT THE AUTHORS AND THEIR DOGS

Palla di Neve, "Nevi," is an American Eskimo dog, all white with black points. The AKC refers to this breed as the 'dog beautiful' and that it is! The man selling Nevi asked Jodi one favor -- that Nevi not be called Snowball, since he believed a great many American Eskimo dogs have that name. At the time of the purchase, Jodi's husband was studying Italian and, out of curiosity, she asked him to translate the word, 'snowball'. When he told her the translation, she thought it sounded pretty and decided to use it. When she returned to pick up Nevi, the man asked what she named him and she replied, "Palla di Neve". He exclaimed, "Thank goodness you didn't call him Snowball!"

Jodi Alessandrini is married and has two daughters. She owns and operates a talent agency and writes and produces murder mystery events. She has written numerous scripts but this is her first book. Her love of animals and inspiration from Nevi prompted her to write the book with her best friend, Kathy.

Besides Nevi, Jodi has a beautiful and very sweet Golden Retriever/Cocker Spaniel named Katie that she rescued from a busy intersection. She also has a cat, Miss Florida, that she rescued while on vacation (more about that in the next book, KITTEN KABOODLE).

Kathy Kinser delights in creating humorous poetry and stories for birthdays or parties. "There is a truly funny side to most human activity. Some of the best humor comes from ordinary everyday events," she says.

Kathy enjoys an active membership in The P.E.O. Sisterhood and The Women's Symphony Guild. She has recently completed a three year term on the Board of Directors of The Sister Cities Association of Springfield. Her hobbies are paragliding and riding monster roller coasters with husband, Dave.

Kathy's house pets are Dale, an affectionate fluffy black cat that Kathy adopted several years ago; and Chocolate Chip, the Chocolate Labrador pictured here. Chip's friendly disposition, trusting nature and expressive golden eyes are just three of the endearing qualities that make him irresistible.

PHOTOS BY: STUDIO 131, PHOTOGRAPHY, SPRINGFIELD, ILLINOIS
PHOTO RESOURCE CENTER, SPRINGFIELD, ILLINOIS

DOG SITTER INSTRUCTIONS FOR THE CARE OF

_____
(MY NAME)

from _____ to _____
(DATE)   (DATE)

My veterinarian's name is _____

Veterinarian's phone number: _____

Veterinarian's address: _____

Emergency veterinary phone number: _____

My owner will be at: _____

My owner can be reached at this phone number, _____

or my owner wishes you to call _____
(NAME)

at _____ if I have any problems.
(PHONE NUMBER)

Location of my supplies:

    Food and water bowls _____

    Food and treats _____

    Daily medications _____

    Toys _____

    Grooming tools _____

    First-aid kit _____

    Leash and collar _____

    Pooper scooper and plastic bags _____

    Bed _____

    Medical records _____

Instructions:

    Feeding _____

    Potty _____

    Exercise _____

    Sleeping _____

    Bathing (location) _____

    Bathing equipment _____

DOG SITTER INSTRUCTIONS FOR THE CARE OF

_____
(MY NAME)

from _____ to _____
      (DATE)   (DATE)

My veterinarian's name is _____

Veterinarian's phone number: _____

Veterinarian's address: _____

Emergency veterinary phone number: _____

My owner will be at: _____

My owner can be reached at this phone number, _____ ,

or my owner wishes you to call _____
                                            (NAME)

at _____ if I have any problems.
     (PHONE NUMBER)

Location of my supplies:

    Food and water bowls _____

    Food and treats _____

    Daily medications _____

    Toys _____

    Grooming tools _____

    First-aid kit _____

    Leash and collar _____

    Pooper scooper and plastic bags _____

    Bed _____

    Medical records _____

Instructions:

    Feeding _____

    Potty _____

    Exercise _____

    Sleeping _____

    Bathing (location) _____

    Bathing equipment _____

DOG SITTER INSTRUCTIONS FOR THE CARE OF

_____
(MY NAME)

from _____ to _____
        (DATE)   (DATE)

My veterinarian's name is _____

Veterinarian's phone number: _____

Veterinarian's address: _____

Emergency veterinary phone number: _____

My owner will be at: _____

My owner can be reached at this phone number, _____ ,

or my owner wishes you to call _____
                                     (NAME)

at _____ if I have any problems.
  (PHONE NUMBER)

Location of my supplies:

    Food and water bowls _____

    Food and treats _____

    Daily medications _____

    Toys _____

    Grooming tools _____

    First-aid kit _____

    Leash and collar _____

    Pooper scooper and plastic bags _____

    Bed _____

    Medical records _____

Instructions:

    Feeding _____

    Potty _____

    Exercise _____

    Sleeping _____

    Bathing (location) _____

    Bathing equipment _____

DOG SITTER INSTRUCTIONS FOR THE CARE OF

_____
(MY NAME)

from _____ to _____
   (DATE)   (DATE)

My veterinarian's name is _____

Veterinarian's phone number: _____

Veterinarian's address: _____

Emergency veterinary phone number: _____

My owner will be at: _____

My owner can be reached at this phone number, _____ ,

or my owner wishes you to call _____
                                          (NAME)
at _____ if I have any problems.
        (PHONE NUMBER)

Location of my supplies:

   Food and water bowls _____

   Food and treats _____

   Daily medications _____

   Toys _____

   Grooming tools _____

   First-aid kit _____

   Leash and collar _____

   Pooper scooper and plastic bags _____

   Bed _____

   Medical records _____

Instructions:

   Feeding _____

   Potty _____

   Exercise _____

   Sleeping _____

   Bathing (location) _____

   Bathing equipment _____

DOG SITTER INSTRUCTIONS FOR THE CARE OF

_____
(MY NAME)

from _____ to _____
      (DATE)   (DATE)

My veterinarian's name is _____

Veterinarian's phone number: _____

Veterinarian's address: _____

Emergency veterinary phone number: _____

My owner will be at: _____

My owner can be reached at this phone number, _____ ,

or my owner wishes you to call _____
                               (NAME)

at _____ if I have any problems.
   (PHONE NUMBER)

Location of my supplies:

    Food and water bowls _____

    Food and treats _____

    Daily medications _____

    Toys _____

    Grooming tools _____

    First-aid kit _____

    Leash and collar _____

    Pooper scooper and plastic bags _____

    Bed _____

    Medical records _____

Instructions:

    Feeding _____

    Potty _____

    Exercise _____

    Sleeping _____

    Bathing (location) _____

    Bathing equipment _____

DOG SITTER INSTRUCTIONS FOR THE CARE OF

_____
(MY NAME)

from _____ to _____
      (DATE)   (DATE)

My veterinarian's name is _____

Veterinarian's phone number: _____

Veterinarian's address: _____

Emergency veterinary phone number: _____

My owner will be at: _____

My owner can be reached at this phone number, _____ ,

or my owner wishes you to call _____
                                      (NAME)

at _____ if I have any problems.
    (PHONE NUMBER)

Location of my supplies:

    Food and water bowls _____

    Food and treats _____

    Daily medications _____

    Toys _____

    Grooming tools _____

    First-aid kit _____

    Leash and collar _____

    Pooper scooper and plastic bags _____

    Bed _____

    Medical records _____

Instructions:

    Feeding _____

    Potty _____

    Exercise _____

    Sleeping _____

    Bathing (location) _____

    Bathing equipment _____

DOG SITTER INSTRUCTIONS FOR THE CARE OF

_____
(MY NAME)

from _____ to _____
        (DATE)   (DATE)

My veterinarian's name is _____

Veterinarian's phone number: _____

Veterinarian's address: _____

Emergency veterinary phone number: _____

My owner will be at: _____

My owner can be reached at this phone number, _____ ,

or my owner wishes you to call _____
                                                         (NAME)

at _____ if I have any problems.
        (PHONE NUMBER)

Location of my supplies:

　　　Food and water bowls _____

　　　Food and treats _____

　　　Daily medications _____

　　　Toys _____

　　　Grooming tools _____

　　　First-aid kit _____

　　　Leash and collar _____

　　　Pooper scooper and plastic bags _____

　　　Bed _____

　　　Medical records _____

Instructions:

　　　Feeding _____

　　　Potty _____

　　　Exercise _____

　　　Sleeping _____

　　　Bathing (location) _____

　　　Bathing equipment _____

DOG SITTER INSTRUCTIONS FOR THE CARE OF

_____
(MY NAME)

from _____ to _____
        (DATE)   (DATE)

My veterinarian's name is _____

Veterinarian's phone number: _____

Veterinarian's address: _____

Emergency veterinary phone number: _____

My owner will be at: _____

My owner can be reached at this phone number, _____ ,

or my owner wishes you to call _____
                                              (NAME)
at _____ if I have any problems.
        (PHONE NUMBER)

Location of my supplies:

    Food and water bowls _____

    Food and treats _____

    Daily medications _____

    Toys _____

    Grooming tools _____

    First-aid kit _____

    Leash and collar _____

    Pooper scooper and plastic bags _____

    Bed _____

    Medical records _____

Instructions:

    Feeding _____

    Potty _____

    Exercise _____

    Sleeping _____

    Bathing (location) _____

    Bathing equipment _____

DOG KENNEL INSTRUCTIONS FOR THE CARE OF

_____
(MY NAME)

from _____ to _____
       (DATE)   (DATE)

My veterinarian's name is _____

Veterinarian's phone number: _____

Veterinarian's address· _____

Emergency veterinary phone number: _____

My owner will be at: _____

My owner can be reached at this phone number, _____

or my owner wishes you to call _____
                                       (NAME)

at_____ if I have any problems.
      (PHONE NUMBER)

Special instructions: _____
_____
_____
_____
_____

I am bringing the following toys and supplies: _____
_____
_____

DOG KENNEL INSTRUCTIONS FOR THE CARE OF

_____
(MY NAME)

from _____ to _____
       (DATE)   (DATE)

My veterinarian's name is _____

Veterinarian's phone number: _____

Veterinarian's address: _____

Emergency veterinary phone number: _____

My owner will be at: _____

My owner can be reached at this phone number: _____ ,

or my owner wishes you to call _____
                                         (NAME)

at _____ if I have any problems.
      (PHONE NUMBER)

Special instructions: _____
_____
_____
_____

I am bringing the following toys and supplies: _____
_____
_____

DOG KENNEL INSTRUCTIONS FOR THE CARE OF

_____
(MY NAME)

from _____ to _____
(DATE)   (DATE)

My veterinarian's name is _____

Veterinarian's phone number: _____

Veterinarian's address: _____

Emergency veterinary phone number: _____

My owner will be at: _____

My owner can be reached at this phone number, _____

or my owner wishes you to call _____
(NAME)

at_____ if I have any problems.
(PHONE NUMBER)

Special instructions: _____

_____

_____

_____

I am bringing the following toys and supplies: _____

_____

_____

DOG KENNEL INSTRUCTIONS FOR THE CARE OF

_____
(MY NAME)

from _____ to _____
(DATE)   (DATE)

My veterinarian's name is _____

Veterinarian's phone number: _____

Veterinarian's address: _____

Emergency veterinary phone number: _____

My owner will be at: _____

My owner can be reached at this phone number: _____ ,

or my owner wishes you to call _____
(NAME)

at _____ if I have any problems.
(PHONE NUMBER)

Special instructions: _____

_____

_____

_____

I am bringing the following toys and supplies: _____

_____

_____

DOG KENNEL INSTRUCTIONS FOR THE CARE OF

_____
(MY NAME)

from _____ to _____
      (DATE)   (DATE)

My veterinarian's name is _____

Veterinarian's phone number: _____

Veterinarian's address: _____

Emergency veterinary phone number: _____

My owner will be at: _____

My owner can be reached at this phone number, _____

or my owner wishes you to call _____
                                         (NAME)

at_____ if I have any problems.
      (PHONE NUMBER)

Special instructions: _____

_____

_____

_____

I am bringing the following toys and supplies: _____

_____

_____

DOG KENNEL INSTRUCTIONS FOR THE CARE OF

_____
(MY NAME)

from _____ to _____
      (DATE)   (DATE)

My veterinarian's name is _____

Veterinarian's phone number: _____

Veterinarian's address: _____

Emergency veterinary phone number: _____

My owner will be at: _____

My owner can be reached at this phone number:_____

or my owner wishes you to call _____
                                         (NAME)

at _____ if I have any problems.
      (PHONE NUMBER)

Special instructions: _____

_____

_____

_____

I am bringing the following toys and supplies: _____

_____

_____

DOG KENNEL INSTRUCTIONS FOR THE CARE OF

_____
(MY NAME)

from _____ to _____
      (DATE)   (DATE)

My veterinarian's name is _____

Veterinarian's phone number: _____

Veterinarian's address· _____

Emergency veterinary phone number: _____

My owner will be at: _____

My owner can be reached at this phone number, _____

or my owner wishes you to call _____
                                             (NAME)

at_____ if I have any problems.
          (PHONE NUMBER)

Special instructions: _____

_____

_____

_____

I am bringing the following toys and supplies: _____

_____

_____

DOG KENNEL INSTRUCTIONS FOR THE CARE OF

_____
(MY NAME)

from _____ to _____
      (DATE)   (DATE)

My veterinarian's name is _____

Veterinarian's phone number: _____

Veterinarian's address: _____

Emergency veterinary phone number: _____

My owner will be at: _____

My owner can be reached at this phone number:_____ ,

or my owner wishes you to call _____
                                             (NAME)

at _____ if I have any problems.
           (PHONE NUMBER)

Special instructions: _____

_____

_____

_____

I am bringing the following toys and supplies: _____

_____

_____

To order a **PUPPY STUFF HANG-UP**, send a check or money order payable to PALLACHIP PUBLISHING and this completed form to: PALLACHIP PUBLISHING, P.O. BOX 9677, SPRINGFIELD, IL 62791-9677. The price per hang-up is $ ___14.95___ .

YOUR NAME   (PLEASE PRINT)

ADDRESS (no deliveries to P.O. Boxes or

outside the continental U.S.)

CITY/STATE/ZIP

DAYTIME PHONE (_____)_____

(Photo by Studio 131, Springfield, IL.)

Please send _____ Hang-ups @ $ __14.95__ each $ _____

Illinois residents add $____1.09____ Sales tax per Hang-up $ _____

Shipping and handling @ $_____ per Hang-up $ _____
See Chart A on page 159

Total order (Allow three (3) weeks for delivery.) $ _____

To order a **PUPPY STUFF TOY BOX**, send a check or money order payable to PALLACHIP PUBLISHING and this completed form to: PALLACHIP PUBLISHING, P.O. BOX 9677, SPRINGFIELD, IL 62791-9677. The price per toy box is $____34.95____ .

YOUR NAME   (PLEASE PRINT)

ADDRESS (no deliveries to P.O. Boxes or

outside the continental U.S.)

CITY/STATE/ZIP

DAYTIME PHONE (_____)_____

(Photo by Studio 131, Springfield, IL.)

Please send_____Toy Boxes @ $ __34.95__ each $ _____

Illinois residents add $__2.53__ Sales tax per toy box $ _____

Shipping and handling @ $_____per toy box $ _____
See Chart B on page 159

Total order (Allow three (3) weeks for delivery.) $ _____

ORDER FORM

To order additional copies of **PUPPY STUFF,** send a check or money order payable to PALLACHIP PUBLISHING and this completed form to: PALLACHIP PUBLISHING, P.O. BOX 9677, SPRINGFIELD, IL 62791-9677. The price per book is $_____24.95_____.

YOUR NAME _____
(PLEASE PRINT)

ADDRESS _____
(no deliveries to P.O. Boxes or outside the continental U.S.)

_____

CITY/ZIP/STATE _____

DAYTIME PHONE (_____)_____

Please send _____ copies @ $ __24.95__ each $ _____

Illinois residents add $ __1.55__ Sales tax per book $ _____

Shipping and handling   @ $ __3.00__ per book $ _____

Total order $ _____
Allow three (3) weeks for delivery.

Chart A — Shipping and Handling for Puppy Stuff Hang-ups

Zone 1	Zone 2	Zone 3	Zone 4	Zone 5
$3.38	$4.10	$5.19	$5.56	$5.95

Chart B — Shipping and Handling for Puppy Stuff Toy Boxes

Zone 1	Zone 2	Zone 3	Zone 4	Zone 5
$4.37	$5.79	$7.96	$10.03	$12.52

STATE/ZONE CHART

State	Zone	State	Zone	State	Zone	State	Zone	State	Zone
Alabama	2	Illinois	1	Minnesota	2	N. Carolina	4	Texas	3
Arizona	4	Indiana	1	Mississippi	2	N. Dakota	3	Utah	4
Arkansas	2	Iowa	1	Missouri	1	Ohio	3	Vermont	5
California	5	Kansas	3	Montana	5	Oklahoma	3	Virginia	4
Colorado	3	Kentucky	1	Nebraska	3	Oregon	5	Washington	5
Connecticut	4	Louisiana	3	Nevada	4	Pennsylvania	4	West Virginia	4
Delaware	4	Maine	5	New Hamsh.	5	Rhode Island	5	Wisconsin	1
Florida	4	Maryland	4	New Jersey	4	S. Carolina	4	Wyoming	3
Georgia	4	Mass.	5	New Mexico	4	S. Dakota	3		
Idaho	5	Michigan	3	New York	4	Tennessee	1		